W9-BKI-035

IOWA
TRIVIA

IOWA TRIVIA

COMPILED BY JANICE BECK STOCK, ALAN BECK, AND KEN BECK

Rutledge Hill Press
Nashville, Tennessee

Copyright © 1996 by Janice Beck Stock, Alan Beck, and Ken Beck. All rights reserved. Written permission must be secured from the publisher to use or reproduce any part of this book, except for brief quotations in critical reviews and articles.

Published in Nashville, Tennessee, by Rutledge Hill Press, 211 Seventh Avenue North, Nashville, Tennessee 37219. Distributed in Canada by H. B. Fenn & Company, Ltd., 1090 Lorimar Drive, Mississauga, Ontario L5S 1R7.

Typography by D&T/Bailey Typesetting, Inc., Nashville, Tennessee.

Library of Congress Cataloging-in-Publication Data
Stock, Janice Beck, 1954–
    Iowa trivia / compiled by Janice Beck Stock, Alan Beck, and Ken Beck.
        p. cm.
    ISBN 1-55853-396-6 (pbk.)
    1. Iowa—Miscellanea. I. Beck, Alan, 1958– . II. Beck, Ken, 1951– . III. Title.
F621.S84   1996
977.7—dc20   96-2093
                                                    CIP

Printed in the United States of America.
2 3 4 5 6 7 8 9 — 99 98 97 96

PREFACE

This book was designed to be informative, interesting, and entertaining. We hope to give fellow Iowans a greater awareness of their state's rich heritage and continuing unique role. We also hope it will entice others to come visit and learn more about the Hawkeye State.

But whoever you are and wherever you're from, it is our wish that it will make you smile and thereby prove true the claim of the state's division of tourism.

First question: What is the current Iowa Division of Tourism slogan?

Answer: Iowa—you make me smile.

To the wonderful people of the state of Iowa

TABLE OF CONTENTS

GEOGRAPHY

C H A P T E R   O N E

Q. The state's geographic center is in what county?

A. Story County.

Q. For how many miles does the Des Moines River flow through Iowa?

A. 485.

Q. What is Iowa's only town on an island?

A. Sabula.

Q. Where can one find Snake Alley, designated by *Ripley's Believe It or Not!* as the crookedest street in the world?

A. Burlington.

Q. What was the original name of Des Moines?

A. Fort Raccoon.

Q. The Nodaway, Middle Nodaway, and East Nodaway Rivers in southwest Iowa take their name from the Indian word for what reptile?

A. Rattlesnake.

Q. The name of what town in Clayton County honors a bedouin emir of Algeria?

A. Elkader.

Q. Where is the home of "the World's Largest Strawberry"?

A. Strawberry Point.

Q. What are the five largest natural lakes in Iowa?

A. East Okoboji, West Okoboji, Clear, Spirit, and Storm.

Q. What popular ice cream treat was invented in Onawa in 1920?

A. Eskimo Pie.

Q. How many counties are in Iowa?

A. Ninety-nine.

Q. What is Iowa's largest county by land area?

A. Kossuth.

Q. What city is known both as "the Pearl of the Mississippi" and as "Melon City"?

A. Muscatine.

Q. What is the only village in the Amana Colonies without the word Amana in it?

A. Homestead.

Q. What two towns were named for the first letters of the names of six pretty women who accompanied railroad officials to the sites?

A. Le Mars and Delmar.

Q. John I. Blair, builder of the Chicago and Northwestern and director of seventeen railroads, has what two towns in Iowa named for him?

A. Blairstown and Blairsburg.

Q. What town's motto is *In Deo spes nostra et refugium* (In God is our hope and refuge)?

A. Pella.

Q. In the past, what was the greatest number of covered bridges at one time found in Madison County?

A. Nineteen.

Q. Originally, what was the name of Atlantic supposed to be?

A. Pacific.

Q. What is the most common translation of the Indian word *Iowa*?

A. "Beautiful land."

Q. The third-largest insurance center in the world, what city is home to more than fifty insurance companies?

A. Des Moines.

Q. What two explorers met with the Missouri and Oto Indians at Council Bluffs in 1804?

A. Lewis and Clark.

Q. Between which two towns was the birthplace of Buffalo Bill Cody?

A. LeClaire and McCausland.

Q. The state's first interurban concrete highway connected what two cities?

A. Clear Lake and Mason City.

Q. Since 1915 the nickname of what two towns has been "the Golden Buckle of the Corn Belt"?

A. Rockwell City and Dysart.

Q. The state's smallest city park is situated in the middle of the road in what town?

A. Hiteman.

Q. Where is the oldest water tower still in service in Iowa?

A. Scranton.

———◆———

Q. Every street in what town is named for an event or person in the life of the admiral for whom it was named?

A. Farragut (Adm. David G. Farragut).

———◆———

Q. What is the name of the most scenic route through the Des Moines Recreational River and Greenbelt area, which passes through nine counties along the Des Moines, Boone, and Raccoon Rivers?

A. Dragoon Trail.

———◆———

Q. What three rivers create the state's eastern and western boundaries?

A. Big Sioux, Missouri, and Mississippi.

———◆———

Q. What county has the highest elevation in the state at 1,670 feet?

A. Osceola.

———◆———

Q. What is the state's oldest city?

A. Dubuque.

———◆———

Q. Where was Elk Horn's Danish Windmill built?

A. Norre Snede, Denmark.

Q. How large are Iowa townships?

A. Six miles square.

Q. A replica of the *Little Mermaid* statue in Copenhagen Harbor can be seen in what town?

A. Kimballton.

Q. The Boone and Iowa Rivers have their source in Linden Township in what county?

A. Winnebago.

Q. Iowa, which originally had forty-four counties, had how many in 1851?

A. 101.

Q. What town was named after a heavy piece of machinery that fell in a creek and was lost?

A. Cylinder.

Q. The two farms given to Abraham Lincoln for his services in the Black Hawk War of 1832 were near what two present-day towns?

A. Garwin and Denison.

Q. Where was the first public high school in Iowa?

A. Tipton.

Q. What town was named because an early resident, Mrs. James Baker, had a fondness for a Scottish song?

A. Afton ("Flow Gently, Sweet Afton").

Q. In what town is Winnebago Industries located?

A. Forest City.

Q. What trade did the first four settlers of Mechanicsville ply?

A. Mechanic.

Q. What was the only fort ever built by the U.S. government to protect one Indian tribe from another?

A. Fort Atkinson.

Q. The Iowa District was first placed under the laws of the United States in 1834 by being annexed to what territory?

A. Territory of Michigan.

Q. What college of some sixteen hundred students has half of its student body studying abroad?

A. Central University.

———◆———

Q. The golden spike that marked completion of the first transcontinental railroad in 1869 is in what city?

A. Council Bluffs.

Q. In what town are refrigerators, freezers, and microwave ovens manufactured?

A. Amana.

———————◆———————

Q. What town has a statue of "the World's Largest Bullhead"?

A. Crystal Lake.

———————◆———————

Q. The state capital was first in what town?

A. Iowa City.

———————◆———————

Q. What is the only basilica in the United States situated outside of a major metropolitan area?

A. Saint Francis Xavier Basilica in Dyersville.

———————◆———————

Q. Of the original twelve national cemeteries designated by Congress at the same time as Arlington, which one is in Iowa?

A. Keokuk National Cemetery.

———————◆———————

Q. What famous western lawman lived in Pella from age two to sixteen?

A. Wyatt Earp.

———————◆———————

Q. What school was designated by the state legislature in 1904 to act as a highway commission?

A. Iowa State College.

Q. What town in northeast Iowa has the largest ethnic museum in the United States?

A. Decorah.

Q. The Mormon settlement Rushville became the town of Coonville but is now known by what name?

A. Glenwood.

Q. What is the largest body of water in the state?

A. Rathbun Dam and Reservoir.

Q. What was the former name of Monroe County?

A. Kishkekosh.

Q. What part of the state is known as "the Nursery Capital of the World"?

A. Southwest Iowa.

Q. Iowa became part of the United States after what famous land deal with France?

A. Louisiana Purchase.

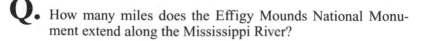

Q. How many miles does the Effigy Mounds National Monument extend along the Mississippi River?

A. Six.

Q. The world's smallest church, Saint Anthony of Padua Chapel, is in what town?

A. Festina.

Q. How many miles wide is Iowa from east to west?

A. 324.

Q. What town in Wright County has Bain-de-la Roche, France, as its sister city?

A. Woolstock.

Q. What Mitchell County town is known as "the City of the Beautiful Maples"?

A. Osage.

Q. What county was named in honor of the only U.S. vice president elected by the Senate?

A. Johnson (Richard Mentor Johnson).

Q. Nealtown was renamed Crawfordsville for a man in what profession?

A. Medical.

Q. What was the nickname of Algona's first school, a dugout in the side of a bluff walled with logs and covered with sod?

A. Gopher College.

Q. What is the largest glacier-created lake in the state?

A. Spirit Lake.

Q. In what ten-year period did the population of Iowa grow by 345.8 percent?

A. 1840–1850.

Q. What is the meaning of Amana, selected from Song of Solomon 4:8?

A. "To remain faithful."

Q. An old glove and sunbonnet factory in Adel is home to what company?

A. Dallas County Brewing Company.

Q. Where is the University of Northern Iowa situated?

A. Cedar Falls.

Q. Dubuque's town clock has been tolling since what year?

A. 1873.

Q. What town had the first courthouse in Iowa?

A. Mount Pleasant.

Q. Iowa has more miles of roads than how many other states?

A. Forty.

Q. The citizens of what town wanted it to be named Missouri Dale when it was incorporated?

A. Modale.

Q. Where is Montauk, the only furnished home built by an Iowa governor that is open as a museum?

A. Clermont.

Q. What county was named after a Hungarian patriot?

A. Kossuth.

Q. What town is "the Home Laundry Appliance Center of the World"?

A. Newton.

Q. What was the name of Julien Dubuque's land claim?

A. The Mines of Spain.

Q. What was the Indian name for Keokuk, meaning "where the water runs shallow"?

A. Puck-e-she-tuck.

Q. What four towns make up the Quad Cities?

A. Bettendorf and Davenport, Iowa, and Moline and Rock Island, Illinois.

Q. What is the state nickname?

A. The Hawkeye State.

Q. In what city is the Bayliss Park Fountain, one of the Midwest's finest lighted, computerized fountains?

A. Council Bluffs.

Q. In the late 1890s, two bank presidents from what town each tried to outdo the other by building a hotel on "his" side of town?

A. Forest City.

Q. The state legislature changed the name of what town by spelling it with a *C* instead of an *S*?

A. Centerville.

Q. What town is in three counties and at the intersection of four townships?

A. Sheldahl.

Q. What is the only county seat in Iowa that is in the exact center of its county?

A. Clarion.

Q. For years the chamber of commerce of what town used the slogan "Next to the largest city in Iowa!"?

A. West Des Moines.

Q. When Iowa became a territory in 1838, which of its twenty-one counties, with 140,000 square miles, was the largest single county ever created in the United States?

A. Fayette.

Q. What town got its name from a music teacher who suggested the town be named for three musical syllables?

A. Ladora.

Q. What city has the only county courthouse with a gold dome?

A. Dubuque.

Q. What was the original name of Fort Dodge?

A. Fort Clarke.

Q. Where is Liberty Hall Historic Center, home of the family of Joseph Smith III, the first president of the Reorganized Church of Jesus Christ of Latter Day Saints?

A. Lamoni.

Q. Where was the first bridge to cross the Mississippi into Iowa?

A. Davenport.

Q. Besides Paris, France, what is the only other city to have its government buildings on an island in the center of the city?

A. Cedar Rapids.

Q. What town in Tama County was originally named Iuka?

A. Tama.

Q. What was the original name of Hamilton County?

A. Yell.

Q. Iowa Falls in Hardin County was once called by what name?

A. Rocksylvania.

Q. Bettendorf went by what name until 1902?

A. Gilberttown.

Q. According to the 1990 census, what is the smallest city in the state, with a population of seven?

A. Donnan (in Fayette County).

Q. What town was home to the state's first newspaper and first bank?

A. Dubuque.

Q. Where is Brucemore, a twenty-one-room Queen Anne-style mansion with fourteen fireplaces?

A. Cedar Rapids.

Q. How many closely united villages compose the Amana Colonies?

A. Seven—East Amana, West Amana, High Amana, Middle Amana, South Amana, Amana, and Homestead.

Q. What town name translated means "there are bears"?

A. Maquoketa.

Q. Railroad owner and avid hunter Charles Whitehead named what three towns along his railway for three of his favorite prey?

A. Mallard, Plover, and Curlew.

Q. With a depth of 136 feet, what is the deepest natural lake in the state?

A. West Okoboji.

Q. What town, named for a Winnebago chief, means "thunder" in the Winnebago tongue and "spirit" in Sioux?

A. Waukon.

Q. What town was named after John I. Blair's dog?

A. Colo.

Q. What kind of animal was Dexter named after?

A. Race horse.

Q. What town was named after the first letters of the surnames of the eight most prominent citizens?

A. Primghar.

Q. Zebulon Pike climbed his first Pike's Peak in Clayton County in what year?

A. 1805.

Q. What town was named for one of its founders, Archer Dumond, and his daughter who was the belle of the community?

A. Belmond.

Q. In April 1994 what city was officially proclaimed "the Ice Cream Capital of the World" by the Iowa legislature?

A. Le Mars.

Q. How many years did it take to survey what is now the state of Iowa?

A. Twenty-three.

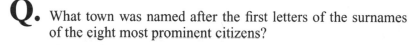

Q. What is the oldest bridge in Madison County?

A. Imes Bridge.

Q. What is the name of the one-hundred-foot white stone obelisk near Sioux City?

A. Floyd's Monument.

Q. The fork of the Raccoon and Des Moines Rivers is the location of what city?

A. Des Moines.

Q. What town was formerly called Bloomington?

A. Muscatine.

Q. In 1834 the Iowa district was divided into how many counties?

A. Two, DuBuque and DeMoines.

Q. Why is Stanton known as "Little White City"?

A. Every house is painted white.

Q. What does the name Pella mean?

A. "City of refuge."

Q. What did pioneers call the double-furrow trail that Alex McCready and his son plowed in 1856 between Fort Dodge and Sioux City?

A. The Great Road.

Q. Burlington was named in honor of another Burlington in what state?

A. Vermont.

Q. Council Bluffs's unusual historic county jail has what nickname?

A. The Squirrel Cage.

Q. What river takes its name from the Indian word for "white potatoes"?

A. Wapsipinicon.

Q. On a direct north-south line between the Lake of the Woods and the Gulf of Mexico, what is the highest point?

A. Iron Mine Hill (in Allamakee County).

Q. Wahkaw County was the former name of what county?

A. Woodbury.

Q. What town received its name because so many of its pioneer settlers were members of the Masonic Order?

A. Mason City.

Q. What town is named for an Indian chief who aided settlers during the Black Hawk War?

A. Decorah.

Q. In 1851 where did a pioneer merchant build a store half in Missouri and half in Iowa?

A. Lineville.

Q. What was Iowa's first national monument?

A. Effigy Mounds.

Q. The town name Titonka is derived from an Indian word meaning what?

A. "Big black," the Sioux name for buffalo.

Q. How did Bloomfield get its name?

A. It was pulled out of a hat.

Q. Iowa's longest and highest bridge crosses what body of water?

A. Red Rock Lake.

Q. What city has a sister city affiliation with Eisenach, Germany, the home of Wartburg Castle?

A. Waverly.

Q. Iowans refer to what section of the state as "the Switzerland of America"?

A. The northeast.

Q. On what campus is the fifty-bell Stanton Memorial Carillon located?

A. Iowa State University.

Q. Named for the German inventor of movable type, what town was misspelled in the plat?

A. Guttenberg.

Q. Where was the first consolidated school established in 1896?

A. Buffalo Center.

Q. During World War I the name Lakota was given to what existing town?

A. Germania.

Q. In 1836 when Michigan became a state, Iowa became a part of what newly created territory?

A. Wisconsin Territory.

Q. Where is the largest Danish settlement in the United States?

A. Elk Horn.

Q. What town's population plummeted from eight thousand to one thousand after the Mormons left in 1852?

A. Kanesville.

Q. The big coal deposit in the area inspired the name of what town in Adams County?

A. Carbon.

Q. What was the first land-grant college in the nation?

A. Iowa State University.

Q. In 1855 the Black Hawk County seat was moved from what original site to Waterloo?

A. Cedar Falls.

Q. What is a simple definition of the word *loess,* as found in the Loess Hills region of western Iowa?

A. Windblown silt or dust.

Q. When it was organized in 1846, the Appanoose County seat was called Chaldea; but when the city was incorporated, its name was changed to what?

A. Centerville.

Q. What town in Cherokee County was named for one of the sons of railroad builder John I. Blair?

A. Marcus.

Q. Between which two rivers is Grinnell situated?

A. Iowa and Skunk.

Q. What town was named for Orrin Sage of Ware, Massachusetts, a banker who helped finance its establishment?

A. Osage.

Q. Low Moor was named for what imported English product that was piled beside the railroad track?

A. Steel rails.

Q. A famous rock inspired the name of what town in Cerro Gordo County?

A. Plymouth.

Q. A young girl who confronted a murderer and saved the lives of her brothers is honored by what county name?

A. Louisa.

Q. Dublin, Ireland, is the sister city to what Iowa town?

A. Emmetsburg.

Q. Markers of what shape are used to designate historical and recreational areas along the Great River Road?

A. Pilot wheel.

Q. A historical section called Czech Village and the National Czech and Slovak Museum are in what city?

A. Cedar Rapids.

Q. For whom was Keokuk named?

A. Sac/Fox Indian chief Keokuk.

Q. What was the first fort in Iowa?

A. Fort Madison.

Q. At sixteen miles, what is the longest natural lake in the state?

A. East Okoboji.

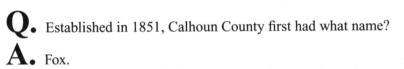

Q. Established in 1851, Calhoun County first had what name?

A. Fox.

Q. Where does Iowa rank in land mass compared to the other forty-nine states?

A. Twenty-fifth.

Q. What town was named after a historian who acknowledged the honor by giving the town fifty books as the nucleus of a library?

A. Bancroft.

Q. What county is known as "the Covered Bridge Capital of Iowa"?

A. Madison.

Q. What does the name *Sioux* mean?

A. "Little snakes."

Q. The last streetcar to operate in the state, Streetcar Number 381, ran between what two towns?

A. Waterloo and Cedar Falls.

Q. What is the distance in miles between Iowa's northern and southern borders?

A. 210.

Q. Risley and Yell Counties were combined to make what county?

A. Webster.

Q. What town was named after Judge John Eckman's daughter?

A. Exira.

Q. What was the original name of West Des Moines?

A. Valley Junction.

Q. In what town is the Old Shot Tower?

A. Dubuque.

Q. Near what town is the largest Amish community west of the Mississippi River?

A. Kalona.

Q. What town takes its name from the Indian word for "swift running water"?

A. Quasqueton.

Q. What fifty-two-mile-long nationally designated trail runs from Waterloo to Cedar Rapids?

A. Cedar Valley Trail.

Q. What town got its name from a large bend in the West Fork of the Des Moines River?

A. West Bend.

Q. What town was renamed for a man who said he would give one thousand dollars for a new church and then never paid up?

A. Rudd.

Q. The 1914 Brenton National Bank building in Grinnell was one of the last structures designed by what famous architect?

A. Louis Sullivan.

Q. What town's name means "rippling waters"?

A. Ottumwa.

Q. The name of what river in southwest Iowa comes from the Indian word meaning "river crossed by boat"?

A. Nishnabotna.

Q. What is the name of the house built by Robert Lucas, the first governor of the Iowa Territory?

A. Plum Grove.

Q. Independence and Summerset were originally suggested as names for what town?

A. Winterset.

Q. The state's lowest elevation point at 480 feet is in what county?

A. Lee.

Q. What six states border Iowa?

A. Illinois, Minnesota, Wisconsin, South Dakota, Nebraska, and Missouri.

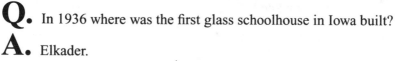

Q. In 1936 where was the first glass schoolhouse in Iowa built?

A. Elkader.

Q. How many covered bridges are there in Madison County?

A. Six.

Q. With a population of 174,700, what is Iowa's second-largest city?

A. Cedar Rapids.

Q. What town name means "white fawn" and was the name of the daughter of a Winnebago chief?

A. Anamosa.

Q. What was the original name given to the Des Moines River by French voyageurs?

A. La Rivière des Moingones.

Q. What trail is currently under development from Cedar Rapids to Burlington?

A. The Herbert Hoover National Recreation Trail.

Q. What does the Sac Indian name Keokuk mean?

A. "Watchful fox."

Q. What town for many years was called Sturgis Falls after the man who founded it?

A. Cedar Falls.

Q. After they received a two-hundred-dollar loan in Des Moines, settlers founded what town?

A. Jefferson.

Q. What town was originally called Altus because, according to railroad surveyors, it was the highest point between Des Moines and Keokuk?

A. Altoona.

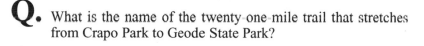

Q. What is the longest bridge in Madison County?

A. Holliwell Bridge.

Q. What is the name of the twenty-one-mile trail that stretches from Crapo Park to Geode State Park?

A. Sho-Quo-Quon Trail.

Q. What county, named in honor of the man who mapped the Iowa District of the Wisconsin Territory, misspelled his name?

A. Lee (Albert M. Lea).

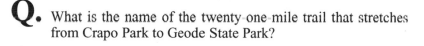

Q. For whom were the towns of Alta and Aurelia named?

A. The daughters of John I. Blair.

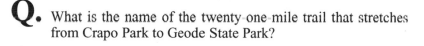

Q. What town name translated means "the last of the beautiful"?

A. Oskaloosa.

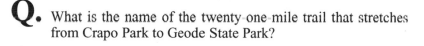

Q. A settlement of Mesquakie Indians can be found near what town?

A. Tama.

Q. Appanoose County was named for a Sac Indian chief whose name means what?

A. "Chief when a child."

Q. What is the meaning of *chicaqua,* the Native American term for an area of the Skunk River in Jasper County?

A. "Offensive odor."

Q. What is the third-largest city in Iowa?

A. Davenport.

ENTERTAINMENT

C H A P T E R   T W O

Q. In the movie *Field of Dreams,* what was Kevin Costner's response to the question, "Is this heaven?"

A. "No. It's Iowa."

Q. Iowa once had fifty drive-in theaters, but how many remained as of 1995?

A. Seventeen.

Q. What pop singing group filmed a live broadcast of their 1995 Cedar Rapids concert?

A. Boyz II Men.

Q. What movie, based on a Johnny Paycheck hit song, was filmed in Des Moines in 1980?

A. *Take This Job and Shove It.*

Q. Indianola's Forrest Tucker starred as Sergeant O'Rourke in what 1960s television western sitcom?

A. *F-Troop.*

Q. What former Des Moines resident starred in *Sheena, Queen of the Jungle?*

A. Irish McCalla.

Q. What Council Bluffs native starred in the title role of the film *Weekend at Bernie's?*

A. Terry Kiser.

Q. Grinnell's Ritchie Haywood is a drummer for what rock group?

A. Little Feat.

Q. What famous brothers' duet of the hits "Bye Bye Love" and "Cathy's Clown" got their professional start in Shenandoah on radio station KMA?

A. Don and Phil Everly.

Q. What NBC News anchorman attended the University of Iowa?

A. Tom Brokaw.

Q. What Academy Award-winning actor in *Cocoon* attended school at Saint Berchman's in Marion and Columbia Academy in Dubuque?

A. Don Ameche.

Q. In what town can one find the Old Home Filler Up and Keep on Trucking Cafe, made famous by Old Home Bread commercials?

A. Pisgah.

Q. What Oscar winner for *From Here to Eternity* and star of her own television show was born in Denison in 1921?

A. Donna Reed.

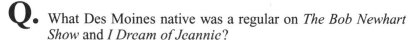

Q. What famous big-band leader was born in Clarinda in 1904?

A. Glenn Miller.

Q. What Des Moines native was a regular on *The Bob Newhart Show* and *I Dream of Jeannie*?

A. Bill Daily.

Q. What Sioux City native played Theodore Cleaver on *Leave It to Beaver*?

A. Jerry Mathers.

Q. What famous late-night television host was born in Corning in 1925?

A. Johnny Carson.

Q. What Burlington native played Bub on *My Three Sons* and Fred Mertz on *I Love Lucy*?

A. William Frawley.

Q. The title of two different hit songs, one by ABBA and the other by Stonewall Jackson, is the same as what Iowa town name?

A. Waterloo.

Q. Who first performed "The Iowa Corn Song" in public in 1912?

A. The Des Moines Shriners.

Q. Who wrote the song "The Little Brown Church in the Vale"?

A. William S. Pitts.

Q. What was the state's first television station?

A. WOC in Davenport, in 1949.

Q. What product was advertised in 1960s television commercials by a man who said, "Nothing is better for thee, than me"?

A. Quaker Oats cereal.

Q. To honor Virginia Christine, television's Mrs. Olson, the Stanton water tower was constructed in the shape of what kitchen appliance?

A. Coffee pot.

Q. What Oscar-winning actor and star of *High Noon* was a student at Grinnell College?

A. Gary Cooper.

Q. Winterset-born film star John Wayne won an Academy Award in 1969 for his performance in what movie?

A. *True Grit.*

Q. On what television series did Sada Thompson, born in Des Moines in 1929, play Kate Lawrence?

A. *Family.*

Q. Where was Roseanne and Tom Arnold's cafe situated?

A. Eldon.

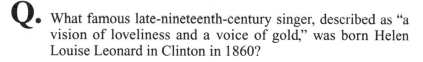

Q. The Iowa State Fair has inspired three films, all with what title?

A. *State Fair.*

Q. Where was jazz great Leon "Bix" Beiderbecke born?

A. Davenport.

Q. What famous late-nineteenth-century singer, described as "a vision of loveliness and a voice of gold," was born Helen Louise Leonard in Clinton in 1860?

A. Lillian Russell.

Q. What Sioux City native played Gopher on *The Love Boat* and also served Iowa's Sixth District in the U.S. House of Representatives?

A. Fred Grandy.

Q. On what television detective show did Hawarden native Hope Emerson play a character named Mother?

A. *Peter Gunn.*

Q. What title did Peggy Lee suggest that Burlington composer Bart Howard use for his song "In Other Words"?

A. "Fly Me to the Moon."

Q. What Miss Universe winner (1957) was from Ottumwa?

A. Carol Morris.

Q. What cowboy actor-singer had a hit with "Sioux City Sue"?

A. Gene Autry.

Q. What role does 1991 Graceland College graduate and Council Bluffs native David Yost play on television's *Mighty Morphin Power Rangers*?

A. Billy, the Blue Ranger.

Q. Based on a Mark Twain novel, what 1974 movie was filmed in Iowa along the Mississippi River?

A. *Huckleberry Finn.*

Q. Riverside claims to be the future birthplace (March 21, 2228) of what fictional character?

A. Capt. James T. Kirk of the USS *Enterprise.*

Q. What was the last name of sisters Lola, Priscilla, and Rosemary, who grew up in Indianola and costarred in a series of movies that began with *Four Daughters* in 1938?

A. Lane.

Q. What pianist got his professional start at Babe's Restaurant in Des Moines and attended Drake University?

A. Roger Williams.

Q. What ABC News correspondent grew up in northeast Iowa and worked at WMT in Cedar Rapids?

A. Richard Threlkeld.

Q. Just before the Prince of Wales became King Edward VII in 1901, what sleight-of-hand expert from Marshalltown taught him a few coin tricks?

A. T. Nelson Downs.

Q. What CNN reporter from Ames is married to television reporter Nancy Loo?

A. Brian Jenkins.

Q. What was the role of Marshalltown's Ruth E. Smith in the 1939 film classic *The Wizard of Oz*?

A. One of the 124 Munchkins.

Q. What animals did Ringling Brothers circus clown Felix Adler use in his act?

A. Pigs.

Q. The 1992 television movie *The Woman Who Loved Elvis* starring Roseanne Barr was filmed in what town?

A. Ottumwa.

Q. What Barbara Stanwyck/Joel McCrea film was shot in Council Bluffs in 1938?

A. *Union Pacific.*

Q. Where did Daniel J. Travanti, star of the television series *Hill Street Blues,* grow up?

A. Dubuque.

Q. During the 1930s and 1940s, what Davenport native appeared in nearly one hundred films, such as *The Sign of the Cross, Northwest Passage,* and *Young Dr. Kildare*?

A. Nat Pendleton.

Q. What University of Iowa graduate played Barney Collier on television's *Mission: Impossible*?

A. Greg Morris.

Q. During the CB radio craze of the 1970s, what was the smash hit song of Audubon's C. W. McCall?

A. "Convoy."

Q. What Council Bluffs native played Elvis Presley's romantic interest in the film *Roustabouts*?

A. Joan Freeman.

Q. What magician built a house in Fairfield?

A. David Copperfield.

Q. What Davenport native portrays Tom Hardy on *General Hospital*?

A. Matthew Ashford.

Q. What Cornell College alumnus composed more than seven hundred popular songs, including "In the Shade of the Old Apple Tree"?

A. Egbert Van Alstyne.

Q. Born in LaPorte City, what children's television star played the straight woman to puppets Kukla and Oliver J. Dragon?

A. Fran Allison.

Q. What Woolstock native played one of the Tarleton twins in *Gone With the Wind* and was television's first Superman?

A. George Reeves.

Q. What Davenport native starred in the television series *MacGruder & Loud*?

A. John Getz.

Q. What song from the musical *The Music Man* has the word *Iowa* in the title?

A. "Iowa Stubborn."

Q. On what date, known as "the day the music died," did Buddy Holly die in a plane crash after he performed in Iowa?

A. February 3, 1959.

Q. Where was Andy Williams of "Moon River" fame born in 1930?

A. Wall Lake.

Q. What television star of *Mrs. Columbo* and *Star Trek Voyager* was born in Dubuque in 1955?

A. Kate Mulgrew.

Q. Where was the boyhood home of puppeteer Bill Baird?

A. Mason City.

Q. What Decorah native played Sharon Gless's mother in the television show *The Trials of Rosie O'Neill*?

A. Georgann Johnson.

Q. In what 1954 horror flick did Waterloo's Julie Adams play the heroine?

A. *Creature from the Black Lagoon.*

Q. What 1950 film was loosely based on the life of jazz cornet great Bix Beiderbecke?

A. *Young Man with a Horn.*

Q. *Entertainment Tonight* host Mary Hart formerly worked for what station in Cedar Rapids?

A. KGAN-TV.

Q. Shot in Council Bluffs and directed by Sean Penn, what 1991 film was inspired by Bruce Springsteen's song "Highway Patrol"?

A. *The Indian Runner.*

Q. What Audubon native sang with Kenny Rogers on the hit song "Ruby, Don't Take Your Love to Town" and later married Roger Miller?

A. Mary Arnold Miller.

Q. In what town did Nick Nolte, star of *Down and Out in Beverly Hills, Lorenzo's Oil,* and the miniseries *Rich Man, Poor Man,* attend elementary school?

A. Ames.

Q. In what Doris Day film can one spot Cedar Rapids native Lois Raymond?

A. *Pillow Talk.*

Q. What Leon native played Peter Kane on *As the World Turns*?

A. Arlen Snyder.

Q. What 1938 film was shot in Anamosa?

A. *Penitentiary.*

Q. Where did Farm Aid VI take place on April 24, 1993?

A. Ames.

Q. What self-proclaimed "Most Famous Hostess in the World" was born in the Keokuk town hall in 1887?

A. Elsa Maxwell.

Q. What Davenport native starred in the films *Lolita, The Flim Flam Man,* and *The Night of the Iguana*?

A. Sue Lyon.

Q. Since what year has there been a municipal band in Oskaloosa?

A. 1864.

Q. What heavy metal band filmed a music video in Cedar Rapids in 1988?

A. The Scorpions.

Q. The 1980 film *Pennies from Heaven* starring Steve Martin and Bernadette Peters was shot in what Iowa city?

A. Dubuque.

Q. Born in Waterloo, what international recording star began her career as a child by winning on *Star Search*?

A. Tracie Spencer.

Q. What actress lived in Randalia and was a model in Des Moines before moving to Hollywood and becoming a regular on *CHiPs*?

A. Randi Oakes.

Q. Author of *The Seven Per-Cent Solution* and *The West End Horror,* what director and writer studied at the University of Iowa?

A. Nicholas Meyer.

Q. What role did Grinnell College graduate Walter Koenig play in *Star Trek*?

A. Ens. Pavel Chekov.

Q. What Des Moines native played trombone with Henry Mancini for many years?

A. Johnny Haliburten.

Q. Wade on *All My Children* was played by what Fort Dodge native?

A. Marlian Fisher.

Q. Famous for his tipsy portrayals, what comedian was a deejay at radio station KBIZ in Ottumwa?

A. Foster Brooks.

Q. What producer of such films as *The Amityville Horror, Love at First Bite,* and *Dr. Phibes* was born in Fort Dodge in 1918?

A. Samuel Arkoff.

Q. Meredith Willson began his professional career playing what instrument with the John Philip Sousa Band?

A. Flute.

Q. What courthouse and its square were the setting for the 1969 Dick Van Dyke film *Cold Turkey*?

A. Winterset.

Q. What film star of *Saint Joan* and *Paint Your Wagon* was born in Marshalltown in 1939?

A. Jean Seberg.

Q. What Des Moines native starred in television's *Tales of the Gold Monkey*?

A. Stephen Collins.

Q. What Keystone Kop comedian and star of television's *Doc Corkle* was born in Oskaloosa?

A. Chester Conklin.

Q. Hampton's Jack Bailey was the host of what daytime television game show in the 1950s?

A. *Queen for a Day.*

Q. Gary Kroeger, a *Saturday Night Live* cast member from 1982 to 1985, was born in what city?

A. Cedar Falls.

Q. What Doobie Brothers drummer was born in Iowa?

A. Keith Knudsen.

Q. What movie included a scene filmed at the Fenelon Place elevator in Dubuque?

A. *F.I.S.T.*

Q. What University of Iowa athlete played Yancy Derringer on television and Tarzan on the silver screen?

A. Jock Mahoney

Q. Dubuque's Richard Bissell wrote the stage and film versions of what show starring Doris Day and John Raitt?

A. *Pajama Game.*

Q. Author, comedian, and actor Steve Allen attended what university?

A. Drake.

Q. What star of *E.T.: The Extra-Terrestrial, Cross Creek,* and *Jagged Edge* earned a bachelor's degree in English at Grinnell College?

A. Peter Coyote.

Q. What former NBC consumer reporter formerly worked at radio station KRNT in Des Moines?

A. David Horowitz.

Q. What was the stage name of the actress, born in Clarinda as Marvel Maxwell, who starred in the films *The Lemon Drop Kid* and *Rock-a-bye Baby*?

A. Marilyn Maxwell.

Q. What *CBS This Morning* host attended Central College in Pella?

A. Harry Smith.

Q. What star of *Blazing Saddles, Young Frankenstein, and Willy Wonka and the Chocolate Factory* graduated from the University of Iowa in 1955?

A. Gene Wilder.

Q. The fictional town of Appleton, Iowa, was the setting for what 1974 television series starring Ronny Cox?

A. *Apple's Way.*

Q. What 1983 film starring Jessica Lange and Sam Shepard was shot in Waterloo?

A. *Country.*

Q. What rock music band filmed a video in Winterset in 1995?

A. The Black Crows.

Q. Sportscaster Greg Gumbel is an alumnus of what college?

A. Loras.

Q. Starring Clint Eastwood and Meryl Streep, what 1995 movie was filmed in and around Winterset?

A. *The Bridges of Madison County.*

Q. What movie star of *The World According to Garp* was born in Marshalltown in 1946?

A. Mary Beth Hurt.

Q. What town provided Meredith Willson the setting for his musical *The Music Man*?

A. Mason City.

Q. How many Ringling brothers were there?

A. Seven. Albert, Otto, Alfred, Charles, and John started out with penny circuses in McGregor. The other two brothers were Henry and August.

Q. What was the first commercial educational television station in the United States?

A. WOI-TV, Iowa State College, 1950.

Q. Who wrote "The Iowa Corn Song"?

A. John T. Beeston and George Hamilton.

Q. On what television series did Cloris Leachman co-star as a character named Phyllis?

A. *The Mary Tyler Moore Show.*

Q. What local talk show host organized the fourth annual International Leisure Suit Convention in Des Moines in March 1992?

A. Van Harden.

Q. What CBS television series, which began in the fall of 1995, has the same title as a Grant Wood painting?

A. *American Gothic.*

Q. What Iowan plays Margo Hughes on *As the World Turns*?

A. Ellen Dolan.

Q. What Disney child star, who appeared in *Song of the South, So Dear to My Heart,* and *Treasure Island,* was born in Cedar Rapids?

A. Bobby Driscoll.

Q. Stuart Margolin, who starred as Angel Martin on *The Rockford Files,* was born in what city?

A. Davenport.

Q. What politician stirred up a national controversy when he attacked network news commentaries during a televised speech from Des Moines on November 13, 1969?

A. Vice President Spiro Agnew.

Q. In 1921 who became known as "the Father of the Iowa Band Law," enabling cities to support a municipal band?

A. Maj. George Landers.

Q. Bill Bailey, who once worked at the Kirkwood Hotel in Des Moines, played what instrument?

A. The banjo.

Q. What Norwalk native appeared in the films *Cleopatra, The Shoes of the Fisherman, Once upon a Time in the West,* and *The Ten Commandments*?

A. John Frederick.

Q. What Ottumwa native was the casting director for *South Pacific* and *Fiddler on the Roof*?

A. Shirley Rich Krohm.

Q. David L. Wolper, producer of *Roots* and *The Thorn Birds,* attended what university?

A. Drake.

Q. The 1968 film *Gaily Gaily,* with Beau Bridges, Melina Mercouri, Brian Keith, and Margot Kidder, was filmed in what city?

A. Dubuque.

Q. What ABC television series starring Craig T. Nelson has filmed scenes several times in Iowa City?

A. *Coach.*

Q. In 1964 what jazz singer and 1982 Grammy winner received a master's degree from the University of Iowa?

A. Al Jarreau.

Q. What type of business did Jean Seberg's parents operate in Marshalltown?

A. A drugstore.

Q. The lives of five brothers from Waterloo who joined the navy were the subject of what 1944 film?

A. *The Fighting Sullivans.*

Q. What star of the 1960s television series *Hazel* was born in Cedar Rapids in 1917?

A. Don Defore.

Q. What was Buffalo Bill's real name?

A. William Frederick Cody.

Q. What Hollywood cinematographer, who was director of photography on *Jaws, Grease,* and *One Flew Over the Cuckoo's Nest,* attended Iowa Wesleyan?

A. Wilmer Butler.

Q. The 1933 film version of *State Fair* starred what famous American humorist?

A. Will Rogers.

Q. In what year did the state's first commercial radio station, WOC, begin operation in Davenport?

A. 1922.

Q. What Joni Mitchell song has an Iowa city as part of its title?

A. "Dry Cleaner from Des Moines."

Q. Where was Sharon Farrell, who plays Flo Webster on *The Young and Restless,* born?

A. Sioux City.

Q. On what television series did Des Moines native David Anthony Higgins portray Joe Farrell?

A. *Ellen.*

Q. What actor, who played Benjamin Horne on *Twin Peaks,* was born in Avoca and starred in the films *The Diary of Anne Frank* and *West Side Story?*

A. Richard Beymer.

Q. What Creston native played receptionist Carol Kester on *The Bob Newhart Show?*

A. Marcia Wallace.

Q. In *It's a Wonderful Life,* what was the first name of the character portrayed by Iowa's Donna Reed?

A. Mary.

Q. What Clinton native was the head clown for the Ringling Brothers circus and from 1919 to 1946 never missed a performance?

A. Felix Adler.

Q. What comedian, writer, and actor born in Ottumwa was once married to Roseanne Barr?

A. Tom Arnold.

Q. What graduate of Central College has anchored ABC's *Good Morning, America* and hosted *Timeline*?

A. Steve Bell.

Q. Annabeth Gish, star of *Mystic Pizza, Wyatt Earp,* and *Desert Bloom,* attended what high school in Cedar Falls?

A. Northern University High School.

Q. What Monroe County native became a cartoonist for Disney and worked on *Peter Pan, Cinderella, The Lady and the Tramp,* and *Alice in Wonderland*?

A. Dan Karpan.

Q. What Pleasantville native appeared in the films *Duel in the Sun, Kiss and Tell,* and *A Guest in the House*?

A. Scott McKay.

Q. Former WMT radio broadcaster Red Rowe was always mentioned by television game show host Chuck Barris at the conclusion of what show?

A. *The Gong Show.*

Q. Carroll native Marian Rees, who worked as a producer on *Miss Rose White, Home Fires Burning, Foxfire,* and *Orphan Train,* graduated from what Des Moines High School?

A. Roosevelt High School.

Q. What 1967 film starring Harry Dean Stanton and John Carradine was shot entirely in the state?

A. *The Hostage.*

Q. In 1984's *Starman,* filmed partially in Cedar Rapids, who starred as an alien needing help from a young widow?

A. Jeff Bridges.

Q. In what Dubuque theater did Al Jolson and Eddie Cantor perform during the days of vaudeville?

A. The Five Flags Theater (formerly the Orpheum).

Q. What was the occupation of Johnny Carson's father when Johnny was born in Iowa?

A. Area manager of the Iowa-Nebraska Power and Light Company.

Q. Born in Council Bluffs in 1884, what film comedian was considered one of the big four of the silent film era along with Charlie Chaplin, Buster Keaton, and Harold Lloyd?

A. Harry Langdon.

Q. Known as "the King of Jazz," what band conductor often spent his summers in Bedford with his grandparents?

A. Paul Whiteman.

Q. What Strawberry Point native was in the films *Back to the Future* and *Top Gun*?

A. David Tolkon.

Q. Born Edward Vance Flanagan in Fort Madison in 1908, what movie star appeared in *Topper Returns* and *Brewster's Millions*?

A. Dennis O'Keefe.

Q. At what age did Donna Reed leave her hometown of Denison by train to go to Hollywood?

A. Sixteen.

Q. What Sioux City native was in the films *Calamity Jane* and *Mister Roberts,* played Philip Marlowe on television, and starred as Tom Horton on *Days of Our Lives*?

A. Macdonald Carey.

Q. What Cedar Rapids native played Jean Smart's television husband on *Designing Women*?

A. Douglas Barr.

Q. Buddy Holly performed his final concert at what venue?

A. The Surf Ballroom.

Q. What is the name of the little boy who "likes it" in the commercials for Life cereal (produced by Iowa's Quaker Oats Co.)?

A. Mikey.

Q. What 1991 film starring Carol Burnett and Michael Caine was shot in Des Moines?

A. *Noises Off.*

Q. What were the first names of the five Cherry Sisters, a vaudeville act so bad they became popular?

A. Ellie, Lizzie, Effie, Addie, and Jessie.

Q. How many cups of coffee can the Stanton water tower hold?

A. 480,000.

Q. Alf Ringling was a juggler and acrobat, but what farm implement could he balance on his chin?

A. Plow.

Q. What was John Wayne's birth name?

A. Marion Robert Morrison.

Q. What 1989 baseball movie starring Kevin Costner was filmed in an Iowa cornfield?

A. *Field of Dreams.*

Q. Soaps actor Mark Pinter, who plays Grant Harrison on *Another World,* was born in what town?

A. Decorah.

Q. What Lourdes native was an accomplished clarinetist whose nicknames included "Jerkwater Jazzmaker" and "King of Korn"?

A. Freddie Fisher.

Q. What Clear Lake native was in the films *Grease, Grease 2,* and *Don't Stop the Music*?

A. Dick Patterson.

Q. LeVar Burton starred in what television movie partially filmed in Clinton?

A. *One in a Million: The Ron LeFlore Story.*

———◆———

Q. During the early 1900s, what famous Chautauqua quartet used "The Church in the Wildwood" as their theme song?

A. The Weatherwax Brothers.

———◆———

Q. A Stephen King horror story served as the basis for what 1983 film shot in Whiting?

A. *Children of the Corn.*

———◆———

Q. What Mason City native was in the movies *National Lampoon's Class Reunion* and *The Incredible Shrinking Woman*?

A. Randolph Powell.

———◆———

Q. What Sioux City native starred in the films *Show Business, You Can't Cheat an Honest Man, Atlantic City,* and *In Old Sacramento*?

A. Constance Moore.

———◆———

Q. What Davenport native plays Sally Gleason on *The Guiding Light*?

A. Patricia Barry.

Q. Who starred as Iowa's Glenn Miller in *The Glenn Miller Story*?

A. James Stewart.

Q. What television series starred former University of Iowa football star Alex Karras as the godfather of Emmanuel Lewis?

A. *Webster.*

Q. Cloris Leachman, who was born in Des Moines in 1926, won an Oscar for what film?

A. *The Last Picture Show.*

Q. What *Melrose Place* star was born in Iowa City?

A. Laura Leighton.

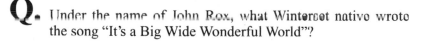

Q. Under the name of John Rox, what Winterset native wrote the song "It's a Big Wide Wonderful World"?

A. John Herring.

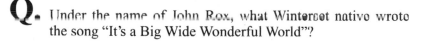

Q. What Keokuk native starred in more than 150 silent and talking films, such as *Little Women, All That Heaven Allows,* and *Forever After*?

A. Conrad Nagel.

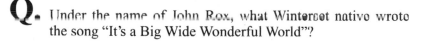

Q. The 1987 film *Miles from Home,* starring Richard Gere, Penelope Ann Miller, Laurie Metcalf, and Helen Hunt, was filmed in what city?

A. Cedar Rapids.

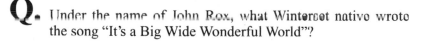

Q. In what year did Donna Reed win her Oscar for *From Here to Eternity*?

A. 1953.

Q. Whose boyhood home in McCausland has buffalo on the grounds?

A. Buffalo Bill Cody.

Q. Where did the Ringling brothers grow up?

A. McGregor.

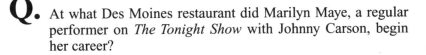

Q. In what town did Buddy Holly, Ritchie Valens, and J. P. "the Big Bopper" Richardson perform their last concert?

A. Clear Lake.

Q. At what Des Moines restaurant did Marilyn Maye, a regular performer on *The Tonight Show* with Johnny Carson, begin her career?

A. Babe's Restaurant.

Q. During the four years that Donna Reed was active in 4-H, for what did she win a blue ribbon at the state fair?

A. Biscuits.

Q. John Wayne's father followed what occupation in Winterset?

A. Pharmacist.

Q. What 1950s television sitcom mom of two boys named David and Ricky was born Harriet Hilliard in Des Moines in 1907?

A. Harriet Nelson.

HISTORY

C H A P T E R   T H R E E

Q. What is the only county seat in Iowa with a bandstand instead of a courthouse in the middle of the square?

A. Oskaloosa.

Q. Because three honey trees were chopped down in a border dispute between Iowa and Missouri, an 1839 incident was known by what name?

A. The Honey War.

Q. Who was the first woman to teach in an Iowa school?

A. Rebecca Palmer.

Q. Billing himself as "the Human Fly," who tried to climb the Davis County courthouse in 1924, fell, and then climbed it successfully in 1932?

A. Henry Poland.

Q. In what year were the first traffic lights installed in Des Moines?

A. 1926.

Q. What self-contained French settlement had the theme "One for all and all for one," and was the longest existing secular, purely communal group in American history?

A. Icaria.

Q. The last battle in Iowa between Native American tribes took place in 1854 between the Sioux and Winnebago near what town?

A. Rolfe.

Q. In 1877 William H. Voss built the first hand-operated washing machine in what city?

A. Davenport.

Q. The nation's first reinforced concrete bridge was built in 1893 three miles from what town?

A. Rock Rapids.

Q. The first wedding in Iowa, that of William Ross and Matilda Morg, took place in what town?

A. Burlington.

Q. Who built the Algona Nativity scene?

A. World War II German prisoners of war.

Q. In 1905 the Jefferson city council passed an ordinance establishing what maximum speed limit for automobiles in the city?

A. Eight miles per hour.

Q. James "Tama Jim" Wilson, secretary of agriculture under three presidents, emigrated from Scotland in 1855 to a farm near what town?

A. Traer.

Q. Who has been nationally honored as "the Mother of 4-H"?

A. Jessie Fields.

Q. What town has a cemetery with a monument for each war, beginning with the Civil War and concluding with Desert Storm?

A. Carroll.

Q. Iowa ranks where among the fifty states for percentage of its population having undergraduate degrees?

A. First.

Q. In what year was the first railroad bridge built across the Mississippi River?

A. 1856.

Q. Grinnell College began as Iowa College in what town?

A. Davenport.

Q. For how many years did Father Doberstein work alone and by hand on the Grotto of the Redemption?

A. Thirty-five (beginning in 1912).

Q. A setting near Nashua was the inspiration for what hymn?

A. "The Church in the Wildwood."

Q. What two Iowa women became first ladies of the nation?

A. Lou Henry Hoover and Mamie Doud Eisenhower.

Q. Iowa's first fire department, the Fire Rescue Company, had only what kind of firefighting equipment available to use?

A. Buckets.

Q. In what year did the first McDonald's restaurant open in Iowa?

A. 1958.

Q. What was the state theme that Gov. Robert Ray adopted in 1970?

A. "Iowa, a place to grow."

Q. In what year did the Iowa State College of Agriculture and Mechanic Arts become Iowa State University of Science and Technology?

A. 1959.

Q. Established in 1867, what was the first life insurance company in Iowa?

A. Equitable Life of Iowa.

Q. From what three nationalities do the majority of Iowans have ancestral roots?

A. German, English, and Irish.

Q. Who founded a packing company in Ottumwa in 1878?

A. John H. Morrell.

Q. Where did Billy Sunday conduct his first revival meeting?

A. Garner.

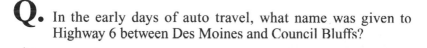

Q. In the early days of auto travel, what name was given to Highway 6 between Des Moines and Council Bluffs?

A. The Great White Way.

Q. During World War II, where was the principal training center for the Women's Army Corps (WAC) located?

A. Fort Des Moines.

Q. Who was the first governor of the state?

A. Ansel Briggs.

Q. To what Indian nation did the Iowa tribe belong?

A. Sioux.

Q. What secret club was begun by six female students at Iowa Wesleyan College in 1869?

A. PEO (it is a philanthropic educational organization, but the actual meaning of the letters is kept secret within the organization).

Q. In what year did Fort Madison publisher James G. Edward promote the nickname "Hawkeyes" for Iowans?

A. 1838.

Q. Whose gang robbed passengers of the Rock Island train west of Adair in 1873?

A. Jesse James.

Q. What town did the Amana Society purchase because it had a railroad?

A. Homestead.

Q. West Branch-born Herbert Hoover was elected president in what year?

A. 1928.

Q. In what year was the first telephone line built in Iowa?

A. 1877.

Q. For whom was Oskaloosa named?

A. Chief Osceola's wife.

Q. What is the state motto?

A. "Our liberties we prize and our rights we will maintain."

Q. What Iowan was secretary of the interior in 1865 under President Andrew Johnson?

A. James Harlan.

Q. Who was the state's first millionaire?

A. Benjamin Franklin Allen.

Q. What company manufactures cotton pickers and grain drills in Ankeny?

A. John Deere.

Q. Who was elected president of the Mormon Church in Kanesville in 1847?

A. Brigham Young.

Q. What explorer selected the site of Burlington for a government fort in 1805?

A. Zebulon Pike.

Q. What is the name of the oldest building on the Iowa State University campus?

A. The Farm House Museum.

Q. What famous foreign leader visited the farm of Roswell Garst in 1959?

A. Nikita S. Khruschev.

Q. At age sixty-six, who was Iowa's oldest governor at the time of his inauguration?

A. Francis M. Drake.

Q. What graduate of Iowa Wesleyan became the first female attorney in the United States in 1869?

A. Arabella Babb Mansfield.

Q. What is the name of the nation's biggest warship, the fifth most decorated of the sixty-one battleships in American history?

A. The USS *Iowa*.

Q. In what war did more Iowa troops, per capita, see action than soldiers from any other state?

A. Civil War.

Q. On what date did Iowa become a state?

A. December 28, 1846.

Q. How old was Kate Shelley when she crawled across a bridge near Moingona during a storm in 1881 to warn a passenger train of a collapsed bridge?

A. Fifteen.

Q. What company manufactured the nation's first tractors?

A. The Hart-Parr Company.

Q. How many types of marble are in the interior of the state capitol'?

A. Twenty-nine.

Q. What Iowan was vice president, secretary of agriculture, and secretary of commerce under President Franklin Roosevelt?

A. Henry A. Wallace.

Q. Who was the first Iowan killed in World War I?

A. Merle Hay.

Q. For how many years was it against the law to establish a bank in the state?

A. Eleven.

Q. Who set a nonstop, cross-country record for flying the mail from Des Moines to Chicago in four hours and forty minutes on October 17, 1914?

A. Billy Robinson.

Q. What national labor leader was born in 1880 in the coal-mining camp of Cleveland, a mile east of Lucas?

A. John L. Lewis.

Q. In 1958 how many one-room, public, rural elementary schools were there?

A. Five thousand.

Q. The name of what Native American tribe in Iowa means "people of the red earth"?

A. Mesquakie.

Q. Who was offered the first governorship of the territory of Iowa but turned it down?

A. Henry Atkinson.

Q. What 1880 graduate of Iowa State founded the League of Women Voters?

A. Carrie Lane Chapman Catt.

Q. What was unique about "the Squirrel Cage" jail in Council Bluffs?

A. Pie-shaped cells rotated.

Q. What two presidents, not native-born, lived in Iowa for part of their adult lives?

A. Ronald Reagan and Richard Nixon.

Q. In 1872 what Davenport native became the nation's first woman high school principal?

A. Phoebe Sudlow.

Q. Where was the first Quaker church west of the Mississippi River founded?

A. Salem.

Q. The administration building for the University of Iowa was originally used for what purpose?

A. State capitol.

Q. Potter's Mill, the state's oldest grist mill, is situated in what town?

A. Bellevue.

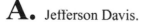

Q. After graduating from West Point in 1828, what Civil War figure operated a sawmill on the Yellow River while serving in the U.S. Army at Fort Crawford?

A. Jefferson Davis.

Q. Until the spring of 1918, the Iowa Savings Bank of Hartley had what name?

A. The German Savings Bank.

Q. Astronaut David Hilmer, actor James Daly, and author Marjorie Holmes are alumni of what college?

A. Cornell College, in Mount Vernon.

Q. What Iowa senator was born in Cummings on November 19, 1939?

A. Tom Harkin.

Q. How much money did Harold Siebens donate to Buena Vista College in 1980, the largest gift per student in the history of higher education?

A. $18 million.

Q. In what year did the Electric Interurban (a trolley) begin running between Mason City and Clear Lake on a regular time schedule?

A. 1897.

Q. In October 1950 six Lost Nation girls made what is said to be the first collection in the United States for what organization?

A. UNICEF.

Q. In 1876 the Des Moines police force was established with how many men?

A. Eight.

Q. Because of scarcity of timber, what substitute material was used for many pioneer homes in northwest Iowa?

A. Sod.

Q. In what year was the state constitution changed to increase the governor's term from two to four years?

A. 1972.

Q. For what is the Reverend John Todd House in Taber famous?

A. It was a major station on the Underground Railroad.

Q. For what Glidden native was the B-29 that dropped the atomic bomb on Hiroshima named?

A. Enola Gay Haggard (mother of the pilot, Col. Paul W. Tibbets).

Q. What was the name of a colony settled in Decatur County in 1859 by a group of Hungarians?

A. New Buda.

Q. Who is the only Iowan to serve as U.S. Speaker of the House?

A. David B. Henderson.

Q. Beginning in 1873, "the Great Grasshopper Invasion" lasted how many years?

A. Six.

Q. The town of Reinbeck derives its name from a German word with what meaning?

A. "Happy stream" or "brook."

Q. Jesse Hiatt of Peru was the first to grow what new fruit?

A. Delicious apple.

Q. Of whom did Gen. Ulysses S. Grant say, "No soldier on the firing line gave more heroic service than she rendered"?

A. Annie Wittenmyer (a wealthy Keokuk matron).

Q. In 1942 an ordnance plant employing nineteen thousand workers was opened by the federal government in what city to manufacture ammunition?

A. Ankeny.

Q. What Iowa governor was in Ford's Theater with Abraham Lincoln when Lincoln was shot?

A. William Milo Stone.

Q. How many Iowans fought in the Civil War?

A. Seventy-six thousand.

Q. What denomination built the first church in Iowa in 1834 in Dubuque?

A. Methodist.

Q. What is the only school in the nation to have its entire campus listed in the *National Register of Historic Places*?

A. Cornell College.

—

Q. What Dexter native was U.S. ambassador to China, Brazil, and Mexico?

A. Edwin H. Conger.

—

Q. Near what town did Gov. Terry Branstad grow up on a farm?

A. Leland.

Q. In 1868 the first law school west of the Mississippi moved to the University of Iowa after being established three years earlier in what town?

A. Des Moines.

Q. In what year did Des Moines become the second city in the nation to have kindergarten as a part of its public school system?

A. 1884.

Q. Founded in 1891, Buena Vista College achieved university status in what year?

A. 1995.

Q. What Mount Pleasant native married Robert Lincoln, the eldest son of Abraham Lincoln?

A. Mary Harlan.

Q. Who were the first two white men to set foot in Iowa?

A. Louis Jolliet and Father Jacques Marquette.

Q. Ames was known by what name until 1866?

A. College Farm.

Q. Where did the word *tractor* originate?

A. Charles City.

Q. Serving from 1923 to 1924, R. W. Cassaday was the first woman to hold what state office?

A. Secretary of agriculture.

Q. In what year was the University of Iowa founded?

A. 1847.

Q. How much salary did Herbert Hoover receive as president?

A. None (he wouldn't accept any).

Q. What former senator's home is within a few blocks of the campus of Iowa Wesleyan?

A. James Harlan.

Q. What son of a famous frontiersman founded Oskaloosa?

A. Capt. Nathan Boone (son of Daniel Boone).

Q. In what year was the first telegraphic message sent in Iowa?

A. 1848.

Q. Iowa began its tradition of holding the nation's earliest presidential caucuses in what year?

A. 1972.

Q. Opened on the north side of Forest City in 1898, what hotel was decorated in black?

A. The Summit.

Q. Opened on the south side of Forest City in 1899, what hotel was decorated in white?

A. The Waldorf.

Q. What Burlington man *suggested* that Iowans call themselves Hawkeyes?

A. Judge David Rorer.

Q. In 1946 what Iowan won the Nobel Peace Prize for his YMCA work and for aiding displaced persons?

A. John Mott.

Q. In what hamlet did former governor William Larrabee and his wife establish a school as their gift to the people?

A. Clermont.

Q. In 1918 where was Iowa's first public junior college established?

A. Mason City.

Q. What type of company did W. A. Sheaffer establish in Fort Madison in 1913?

A. Fountain pen company.

Q. Who was Iowa's last territorial governor?

A. James Clarke.

Q. Where was the Republican Party first organized?

A. Crawfordsville.

Q. How many Iowa counties are named after U.S. presidents?

A. Eleven (Adams, Buchanan, Harrison, Jackson, Jefferson, Madison, Monroe, Polk, Taylor, Van Buren, and Washington).

Q. What was the first public university in the nation to admit men and women on an equal basis?

A. University of Iowa.

Q. What Knoxville resident designed the Iowa state flag?

A. Dixie Cornell Gebhardt.

Q. Bancroft's Greenwood Cemetery is the final resting place of Rev. Ozias A. Littlefield, the founder of what church?

A. The Little Brown Church.

Q. What percentage of Iowa's schools rank above the national average in scholastic achievement?

A. 93 percent.

Q. What was the first city west of the Mississippi to adopt a city manager form of government?

A. Clarinda, Iowa.

Q. What duo robbed the Knierim bank of $272 in 1934?

A. Bonnie Parker and Clyde Barrow.

Q. For how many years did James Wilson serve as the U.S. secretary of agriculture?

A. Sixteen.

Q. What bells in Jefferson chime every quarter-hour?

A. The Mahanay Memorial Carillon.

Q. Waldorf College alumnus John K. Hanson was founder and chairman of the board of what *Fortune* 500 company?

A. Winnebago Industries.

Q. What product was harvested from the Iowa Great Lakes from the 1880s until the 1950s, generating a substantial business?

A. Ice.

Q. The first religious services in George were held in what structure?

A. Train depot.

Q. What is the name of the free student-operated bus system at the University of Iowa?

A. Cambus.

Q. The only pair of brothers to serve in the state legislature from the same county at the same time had what surname?

A. Lynes.

Q. Who was the first teacher in Clear Lake, later a victim in the Spirit Lake Massacre?

A. Eliza Gardner.

Q. What Monroe County town, with a population of about six thousand in 1910, was composed mostly of African Americans?

A. Buxton.

Q. When the first post office was built in Des Moines in 1850, who was appointed postmaster?

A. Hoyt Sherman.

Q. The Iowa income tax on individuals was enacted by the legislature in what year?

A. 1934.

Q. The northernmost Confederate raid of the Civil War occurred in what county?

A. Davis.

Q. In 1943 what wholly new crop were Iowa farmers asked to grow sixty thousand acres of to help the war effort?

A. Hemp.

Q. What was the name of the short-lived colony founded by Abner Kneeland in the late 1830s in Van Buren County, whose inhabitants did not believe in God or religion?

A. Salubria.

Q. At what institution did the first public university school of religion begin?

A. University of Iowa.

Q. Who was described as "the Finest Orator in Congress" after addressing the House of Representatives concerning aid for families of sailors who died in the sinking of the *Maine*?

A. Robert Gordon Cousins.

Q. What college in Epworth is the nation's only four-year Catholic seminary devoted exclusively to training young men for foreign missions?

A. Divine Word College.

Q. As of 1990 what was the population of Iowa?

A. 2.8 million.

Q. What are the three telephone area codes for Iowa?

A. 319, 515, and 712.

Q. What town in Clarke County was named for a Black Drink Seminole warrior?

A. Osceola.

Q. Abbot Bruno laid the foundation of what Trappist monastery near Dubuque in 1849?

A. New Melleray.

Q. As head of the WPA, what Sioux City native spent more than $9 billion during the depression of the 1930s?

A. Harry Hopkins.

Q. What sandwich was devised by Clarinda restaurant owner Bert Gray and named by his chef, who was from Germany?

A. Hamburger.

Q. By 1931 Iowa had how many registered airports?

A. Forty-nine.

Q. The land that became the state of Iowa was acquired during whose presidency?

A. Thomas Jefferson.

Q. In what year was an electric motor first added to a Maytag washer?

A. 1911.

Q. A display of dolls in the state capitol represents whom?

A. The first ladies of Iowa.

Q. What Iowan was secretary of war under President U. S. Grant in 1869?

A. William W. Belknap.

———◆———

Q. The grave of what Native American chief is in downtown Sioux City?

A. War Eagle.

———◆———

Q. How many state universities are in Iowa?

A. Three (Iowa State University, University of Iowa, and University of Northern Iowa).

———◆———

Q. What was the nickname of the Thirty-seventh Iowa Infantry Regiment that was mustered into the Union army on December 15, 1862?

A. The Graybeard Regiment.

———◆———

Q. For how many years did the state have no senators in Washington, D.C.?

A. Two (from late 1846 and into 1848).

———◆———

Q. In 1908 the first women's suffrage parade was held in what town?

A. Boone.

———◆———

Q. In what year did the Amana colonists arrive in Iowa?

A. 1854.

Q. With what religious denomination was Central College affiliated when it opened in 1853?

A. Baptist.

Q. What two men started the Quaker Oats Company in 1873?

A. George W. Douglas and Robert Stuart.

Q. The term *Reynards,* which the French called the Mesquakie Indians, has what meaning?

A. Foxes.

Q. President Franklin Roosevelt and his Republican challenger Alf Landon met in Des Moines on September 3, 1936, to attend what event?

A. The National Drought Conference.

Q. What is the name of the official governor's residence?

A. Terrace Hill.

Q. How many federal defense installations are in the state?

A. None.

Q. When it was completed in the 1920s, what was the name of the first paved, transcontinental highway which crossed Iowa?

A. The Lincoln Highway.

Q. Who was Iowa's first white settler?

A. Julien Dubuque.

Q. Where was the state's first public library established in 1853?

A. Fairfield.

Q. What job did Richard W. Sears, founder of Sears and Roebuck, hold while a resident of Lake Mills?

A. Railroad depot agent.

Q. What college has the oldest undergraduate social-work degree program in Iowa?

A. Wartburg.

Q. What college has a tradition of sending one hundred students on spring service projects to sites around the country and in Mexico?

A. Northwestern, which is in Orange City.

Q. Jessie F. Binford was born in Marshalltown and is a member of the Iowa Women's Hall of Fame for giving her life to help the less fortunate people of what city?

A. Chicago.

Q. What county has the oldest county library system in the state?

A. Scott.

Q. In 1882 Des Moines paved some downtown streets with what unusual material?

A. Cedar blocks.

Q. In 1985 the one-hundred-year-old Bankers Life Company changed its name to what?

A. Principal Financial Group.

Q. What Iowa governor served five terms?

A. Robert Ray.

Q. Families from what country were the first white settlers in Lyon County, settling near the Big Sioux River?

A. Norway.

Q. Salveson Hall of Waldorf College was erected as what building?

A. The Waldorf Hotel.

Q. The Kinsman Monument in Council Bluffs honors veterans of what war?

A. The Civil War.

Q. The first woman to hold a county courthouse job, Emily Stebbins, was appointed deputy recorder and treasurer of Chickasaw County in what year?

A. 1862.

Q. Who was the first governor of the territory of Iowa?

A. Robert Lucas.

Q. Who was the only member of the Lewis and Clark expedition to die during the three-year journey?

A. Sgt. Charles Floyd (who was buried near Sioux City).

Q. What two Iowans have been appointed to the U.S. Supreme Court?

A. Samuel F. Miller and Wiley B. Rutledge.

Q. The oldest college in the state, what private four-year liberal arts college was founded in 1839 by Dubuque's first Catholic bishop?

A. Loras College.

Q. What do the insurance company initials IMT represent?

A. Iowa Mutual Tornado.

Q. What steamboat that sank in the Missouri River in 1866 was raised from the mud in 1965 with much of its cargo preserved?

A. The *Bertrand.*

Q. Because its laborers were paid in groceries and dry goods, what was another name for the failed Lyons-Iowa Central Railroad?

A. Calico Road.

Q. What Bloomfield lawyer was a Civil War brigadier general, editor of the *Davis County Republican,* and twice a candidate for the U.S. presidency?

A. James B. Weaver.

Q. At the turn of the century, what college with just thirteen students decided to expand rather than close, and by 1907 had a new campus complete with a college of liberal arts?

A. University of Dubuque.

Q. The first elevated railroad in the West, a prototype of Chicago's "El," was erected in what city in 1891?

A. Sioux City.

Q. Where was Iowa's first fire department organized?

A. Carroll.

Q. All 122 male students at what college enlisted in the Union army during the Civil War?

A. Bowen Collegiate Institute (now Central College).

Q. What Iowan became secretary of the interior in 1881 under President James Garfield?

A. Samuel J. Kirkwood.

Q. In what year did Iowa become a territory?

A. 1838.

Q. Where is the birthplace of Mamie Doud Eisenhower?

A. Boone.

Q. What railroad builder, Civil War general, and banker built a Victorian mansion in Council Bluffs in 1869?

A. Grenville M. Dodge.

Q. Who was secretary of agriculture in 1920 under President Woodrow Wilson?

A. Edwin T. Meredith.

Q. What is the name of the farm machinery museum in Mount Pleasant?

A. Midwest Old Threshers Museum.

Q. What was Herbert Hoover's religious heritage?

A. Quaker.

Q. In what year was the first law passed by the General Assembly making education compulsory for children between the ages of seven and sixteen?

A. 1902.

Q. The first missionaries to Iowa were of what faith?

A. Roman Catholic.

Q. Who was the youngest man ever elected governor of the state?

A. Terry Branstad.

Q. By what decade were more Iowans living in cities than in small towns or farms?

A. The 1960s.

Q. Teikyo Westmar University in Le Mars was established in 1890 under what name?

A. Western Union College.

Q. How many domes are on the state capitol?

A. Five.

Q. In 1913 what was the first great hydroelectric project completed in the United States?

A. Keokuk Dam.

Q. Who was the first occupant of the present governor's offices in the capitol?

A. Buren R. Sherman.

Q. What is the largest single religious denomination in Iowa?

A. Roman Catholic.

Q. In what year was the Danish Windmill shipped to Elk Horn and rebuilt by community volunteers?

A. 1976.

Q. Approximately how many weddings are held annually at the Little Brown Church in the Vale?

A. 625.

Q. Having organized her own military company for girls, Company G, who was the only woman to graduate from Iowa State College in 1880?

A. Carrie Lane Chapman Catt.

Q. The University of Northern Iowa, previously known as the State College of Iowa and Iowa State Teachers College, was founded in 1876 with what name?

A. Iowa State Normal School.

Q. Who established Iowa's first lending library with his personal collection of more than four hundred books?

A. Elbridge Gerry Potter.

Q. For a few weeks in 1926, all banks in what city failed, making it the largest city in the nation without a bank?

A. Jefferson.

Q. In what year did Cornell College become the first U.S. college to elevate a woman to full professorship with a salary equal to her male colleagues?

A. 1871.

Q. The Mormon Battalion's two-thousand-mile infantry march, the longest one known, began in Council Bluffs in July 1846 and ended six months later in San Diego for service in what war?

A. The Mexican War.

Q. What college in Fairfield opened in 1875 and closed in 1973?

A. Parsons.

Q. What Ida Grove native was elected governor three times and became a U.S. senator in 1968?

A. Harold Hughes.

Q. Millionaire philanthropist Roy Carver spent most of his adult life in what city?

A. Muscatine.

Q. In what year did thirteen hundred European Mormon converts carry their possessions from Iowa City to Salt Lake City in handcarts?

A. 1856.

Q. Before being designated U.S. Highway 65 in 1965, the road that runs two thousand miles from New Orleans to Winnipeg, across Iowa, was known by what name?

A. The Pine to Palm Highway (also the Jefferson Highway).

Q. DeWitt, selected as the Clinton County seat in 1841, was formerly known by what name?

A. Vanderburg.

Q. What town is known as "the Community of Flags" because of its year-round display of the flags of the fifty states?

A. Brooklyn.

Q. The use of what Davenport college facilities by the navy during World War II kept that school alive and its faculty employed?

A. Saint Ambrose.

Q. Who was Iowa's governor during the Civil War?

A. Samuel J. Kirkwood.

Q. What is the name of the diesel engine in Boone said to be the first Chinese steam locomotive in the United States?

A. The *Iowan*.

Q. Maker of printing presses and avionics equipment, what company is the largest employer in Cedar Rapids?

A. Rockwell International.

Q. What Iowan was secretary of agriculture under Presidents William McKinley, Theodore Roosevelt, and William Howard Taft?

A. James Wilson.

Q. What do the four *H*'s of the 4-H symbol stand for?

A. Head, heart, hands, and health.

Q. What was the average age of "the Graybeard Regiment"?

A. Fifty-seven.

Q. Who were Iowa's first two senators?

A. George W. Jones and Augustus Caesar Dodge.

Q. What Native American tribe is thought to be the only one to cede land to Americans and then buy back part of it for a permanent home?

A. Mesquakie.

Q. In what year did a new state law give all children the right to free high school tuition?

A. 1911.

Q. Where was the state's first Roman Catholic church located?

A. Dubuque.

Q. What Waverly woman was the first female to run for public office in Iowa?

A. May E. Francis, who in 1922 ran for superintendent of public instruction.

Q. At what naval air station was Richard M. Nixon stationed in 1942 and 1943?

A. Ottumwa.

Q. What university was founded in the early 1970s as an expression of area pride and is acclaimed as a mythical "University of the Mind"?

A. University of Okoboji.

Q. In what year was Iowa's Historical Department established?

A. 1892.

Q. Who was governor of Iowa from 1943 to 1945 and U.S. senator from 1945 to 1968?

A. Bourke Hickenlooper.

Q. What thirteen-year-old girl was captured by a band of Sioux during the Spirit Lake Massacre of 1857?

A. Abigail Gardner.

Q. For the first time ever, three heads of state met in Iowa on October 21, 1995, representing what three countries?

A. United States, Czech Republic, and Republic of Slovakia.

Q. At the turn of the century, what city was known as "the Cigar-making Capital of the Midwest"?

A. Davenport.

Q. What county was named for a major who was killed in the Mexican War?

A. Ringgold.

Q. Iowa's first governor was inaugurated how many days before President James K. Polk signed the bill of admission bringing the state into existence?

A. Twenty-five (the bill of admission was signed December 28, 1846).

Q. What general from Mason City was wounded in both world wars and from 1925 to 1928 was Dwight Eisenhower's boss as assistant secretary of war?

A. Hanford MacNider.

Q. Who served as an Iowa senator at the same time his father served as a Wisconsin senator, marking the only time father and son have represented different states in the Senate simultaneously?

A. Augustus Caesar Dodge (Henry Dodge was his father).

Q. What president chose Council Bluffs as the eastern junction of the first transcontinental railroad?

A. Abraham Lincoln.

Q. In what year was the state capital moved from Iowa City to Des Moines?

A. 1857.

Q. Who built Terrace Hill in Des Moines in 1869?

A. Benjamin Franklin Allen.

Q. Lyman Dillon plowed a furrow how many miles long from Dubuque to Iowa City?

A. One hundred.

Q. When Iowa's first school, a log cabin built by Dr. Isaac Galland, opened in 1830 in Lee County, what was the teacher's pay?

A. Permission to read Dr. Galland's medical books.

Q. From the laying of the first cornerstone in 1871 until the Supreme Court room was dedicated in 1886, the total cost of the state capitol was $2,873,294.59, with what amount being unaccounted for?

A. $3.77.

Q. What two counties claim that their superintendents of public schools in 1906 designed the official 4-H emblem?

A. Wright and Page.

Q. What was built on the spot where Pope John Paul II gave an address and held a worship service in 1979?

A. The Church of the Land.

Q. A monument to Sgt. Charles Floyd was registered as the first National Historic Landmark by the U.S. Department of the Interior in what year?

A. 1960.

Q. In 1858 what college became the first in Iowa to confer a baccalaureate degree on a woman?

A. Cornell.

Q. What ill Iowa senator had to be carried into the U.S. Senate chambers in order to vote "not guilty" on President Andrew Johnson's impeachment?

A. James W. Grimes.

Q. What was the original name of the Franklin County seat of Hampton?

A. Benjamin.

Q. What Union officer from Burlington inspired the cry "Hold the fort" during a battle at Alatoona, Georgia, in 1864?

A. John M. Corse.

Q. In 1839 the first free public school for physically handicapped children in the nation was opened in what city?

A. Des Moines.

Q. Who was secretary of agriculture under Presidents Warren Harding and Calvin Coolidge?

A. Henry C. Wallace (father of Henry A. Wallace).

Q. How many additional congressional seats was Iowa allotted in 1862 due to population expansion?

A. Four.

ARTS & LITERATURE

C H A P T E R F O U R

Q. What composer was born in Oskaloosa and known as "America's Waltz King"?

A. Frederick Knight Logan.

Q. What Anamosa-born artist painted many of his works while he was a professor at the University of Iowa?

A. Grant Wood.

Q. What town library contains the Mark Twain Center?

A. Keokuk.

Q. What author was born in Storm Lake on May 21, 1944?

A. Janet Dailey.

Q. As of 1995 how many Pulitzer Prizes had been won by staff members of the *Des Moines Register*?

A. Fifteen.

Q. What CBS news broadcaster and *60 Minutes* reporter was born in Dakota City in 1923?

A. Harry Reasoner.

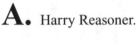

Q. Whom did editor Horace Greeley advise to "Go west, young man, go west"?

A. Josiah Bushnell Grinnell (founder of the town of Grinnell).

Q. Considered to be the father of the skyscraper, what architect designed Clinton's Van Allen Building?

A. Louis Sullivan.

Q. What was the state's first newspaper?

A. *The Du Buque Visitor.*

Q. What magazine was established by Henry Wallace and his son Henry C. Wallace in Des Moines in 1895?

A. *Wallace's Farmer.*

Q. Council Bluffs's bronze sculpture *The Black Angel* is a memorial to whom?

A. Ruth Ann Dodge.

Q. Iowans read more books per capita than how many other states?

A. Forty-nine.

Q. As of January 1995, how many Rhodes scholars had the University of Iowa produced?

A. Eighteen.

Q. What Davenport native, who won a 1931 Pulitzer Prize for the play *Allison's House*, with her husband founded the Provincetown Players and "discovered" Eugene O'Neill?

A. Susan Glaspell.

Q. How much did Grant Wood's painting *Arbor Day* sell for in 1985?

A. $1.25 million.

Q. What museum contains a collection of puppets and marionettes collected by puppeteer Bill Baird?

A. Charles H. MacNider Museum.

Q. For more than thirty years, Riverside World in Iowa Falls has been the world's largest distributor of what product?

A. Bibles.

Q. What publication installed the world's first all-electronic newsroom?

A. The *Quad-City Times.*

Q. Pella's annual celebration, Tulip Time, began in 1935 as an operetta produced by whom?

A. Pella High School students.

Q. What town is named after a Connecticut poet?

A. Sigourney (Lydia Huntley Sigourney).

Q. What Colfax native moved to Tahiti and cowrote *Mutiny on the Bounty* with Charles Bernard Nordhoff?

A. James Norman Hall.

Q. What major American author's grandparents, Ernest and Caroline Hancock Hall, lived near Dyersville more than 130 years ago?

A. Ernest Hemingway.

Q. What Iowa City author is the creator of the character Rambo?

A. David Morrell.

Q. What Clinton native established the University of Iowa's department of political science, the Historical Society's *Palimpsest,* and the *Iowa Journal of History*?

A. Benjamin Shambaugh.

Q. Who shapes the butter sculptures at the Iowa State Fair?

A. Duffy Lyon.

Q. What Grundy County native wrote the novels *Vandemark's Folly, The Hawkeye,* and *The Invisible Woman*?

A. Herbert Quick.

Q. Where is the world's largest collection of hand-carved chains, featuring eighty-three types of wood?

A. Monona Historical Museum.

Q. Wartburg College is the only private college in Iowa to offer a major in what kind of therapy?

A. Music.

Q. In what town did author Paul Hutchins, writer of the *Sugar Creek Gang* series, sit in his car in the driveway of the Evergreen Lawn Cemetery to write?

A. George.

Q. What Cedar Falls native wrote the novel *A Lantern in Her Hand*?

A. Bess Streeter Aldrich.

Q. What Iowa State University graduate and Associated Press correspondent was kidnapped in Beirut on March 16, 1985?

A. Terry Anderson.

Q. From what high school and college did the New York Metropolitan Opera baritone Simon Estes graduate?

A. Centerville High School, and the University of Iowa School of Music.

Q. What landscape painter lived in Burlington for fifty years, painting scenes of the Mississippi River and the oil-on-canvas *View of Burlington*?

A. George Harvey.

Q. What Ottumwa native has investigated UFOs for the government and written books on the subject?

A. Donald Keyhoe.

Q. Ira Levin, author of *Rosemary's Baby* and the stage version of *No Time for Sergeants,* studied writing at what university?

A. Drake.

Q. What Des Moines native and editor of the *Palimpsest* wrote biographies of Robert Lucas, John Chambers, and George Wallace Jones?

A. John C. Parish.

Q. In 1971 an Obie Award went to what Dubuque native for the play *The Basic Training of Pavlo Hummel* and a Tony Award for *Sticks and Bones*?

A. David William Rabe.

Q. The only artist to win the Federal Duck Stamp competition five times was what Arnolds Park native?

A. Maynard Reece.

Q. The horror novels *Zebra's Sweet Revenge, Wild Car,* and *Darksong* were written by what Everly resident?

A. Jean Simon.

Q. What Keosauqua native and novelist saw his books *One Destiny* and *State Fair* turned into films?

A. Phil Stong.

Q. Where was Robert James Waller, author of *The Bridges of Madison County,* born?

A. Rockford.

Q. During the 1920s, what writer from Cedar Rapids was famous for the satires he wrote about New Yorkers?

A. Carl Van Vechten.

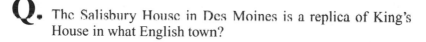

Q. The Salisbury House in Des Moines is a replica of King's House in what English town?

A. Salisbury.

Q. University of Iowa alumnus Mildred Wirt Benson was the creator of what mystery series for young people?

A. *Nancy Drew.*

Q. An Iowa town and county were both named for what Swedish novelist?

A. Bremer (Frederika).

Q. What city does the Des Moines Metro Opera call home?

A. Indianola.

Q. In 1937 Cowles Publishing of Des Moines began what new magazine?

A. *Look.*

Q. With what city are authors Richard Bach *(Jonathan Livingston Seagull)* and Edna Ferber *(Giant)* associated?

A. Ottumwa.

Q. Who was the *Des Moines Register*'s editorial cartoonist before Brian Duffy?

A. Frank Miller.

Q. Who sculpted the *Chief Wapello* statue at the courthouse in Ottumwa?

A. Nellie Verne Walker.

Q. The first written reference to *Iowa* was in the title of a book written by whom?

A. Albert M. Lea *(Notes on the Wisconsin Territory; Particularly with Reference to the Iowa District, or Black Hawk Purchase).*

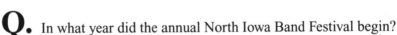

Q. In what year did the annual North Iowa Band Festival begin?

A. 1936.

Q. What type of palace was used to advertise the fertile fields of southwest Iowa from 1889 to 1892?

A. Bluegrass.

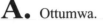

Q. For what novel did Iowa resident Edna Ferber win a 1925 Pulitzer Prize?

A. *So Big.*

Q. What circus composer and musician lived in Fort Dodge from 1919 until his death in 1971?

A. Karl King.

Q. For what book did Keokuk's Cornelia Meigs win the 1934 Newbery Medal for distinguished contribution to American literature for children?

A. *Invincible Louisa.*

Q. What was the occupation of the father of sculptor Nellie Verne Walker, who was born in Red Oak, grew up in Moulton, and was influenced by his work?

A. Tombstone maker.

———◆———

Q. What writer, born near Le Mars in 1927, tells about his early years in Iowa in his book *We Have All Gone Away*?

A. Curtis Harnack.

———◆———

Q. What is the state song?

A. "The Song of Iowa."

———◆———

Q. What Lyons native won the 1970 Pulitzer Prize in journalism for commentary and wrote *Mighty Mississippi: Biography of a River* in 1982?

A. Marquis Childs.

Q. What author and her family lived from 1876 to 1877 in a hotel in Burr Oak?

A. Laura Ingalls Wilder.

Q. What is the state's largest daily newspaper?

A. The *Des Moines Register.*

Q. Grant Wood designed nine murals depicting phases of agriculture for what building at Iowa State College?

A. The library.

Q. As of 1995 the University of Iowa had produced how many Pulitzer Prize winners?

A. Twelve (Robert Olen Butler, in 1993, was the most recent).

Q. What was the birthplace of the art calendar industry in 1888?

A. Red Oak.

Q. What author, born in Storm Lake, is known for her spiritual writing and such novels as *Three from Galilee* and *The Messiah*?

A. Marjorie Holmes.

Q. Iowa State University faculty members Lee Hadley and Ann Irwin cowrote ten novels for young adults under what pseudonym?

A. Hadley Irwin.

Q. What Cedar Rapids poet established the International Writing Program and served as director of the renowned Iowa Writers' Workshop at the University of Iowa?

A. Paul Engle.

Q. While learning her craft in Earlville, what writer kept bees for a living?

A. Ruth Sukow.

Q. Situated in Garrison, what rural professional theater company has received national recognition?

A. Old Creamery Theater.

Q. What attributes does the Quaker Man symbolize on Quaker Oats products?

A. Quality, purity, and honesty.

Q. Iowa's only preprofessional ballet company is in what city?

A. Clinton.

Q. What was the unusual shape of the boyhood home of George Gallup in Jefferson?

A. Octagonal.

Q. What Graceland College graduate and staffer for the *Village Voice* won the 1981 Pulitzer Prize in journalism for feature writing and also wrote the novel *Mob Girl: A Woman's Life in the Underworld*?

A. Teresa Carpenter.

Q. What Jesup native was held hostage in Iran for 444 days, then returned home in 1981 to write the book *Guest of the Revolution*?

A. Kathryn Koob.

Q. What Cedar Falls resident wrote the book *Sleeping with the Enemy*?

A. Nancy Price.

Q. Before becoming an actor or politician, Ronald Reagan wrote a sports column for a newspaper in what Iowa city?

A. Des Moines.

Q. What Pella native was a publisher of the *Saturday Evening Post*?

A. Cory Synhorst Servass.

Q. What Sioux City native, who grew up in Mason City, wrote the books *No Greener Meadows* and *The Girl in the Spike-Heeled Shoes*?

A. Martin Yoseloff.

Q. In what town can one see a Gutenberg Bible facsimile?

A. Guttenberg.

Q. University of Iowa alumnus Max A. Collins Jr. became the writer of what comic strip in 1977?

A. *Dick Tracy.*

Q. Originally supposed to be named after its founder, W. P. Harmon, what town was instead named after Sir Walter Scott novels because of a slip of the tongue at the naming ceremony?

A. Waverly.

Q. What magazine did Des Moines's Meredith Publishing Company start publishing in 1924?

A. *Better Homes and Gardens.*

Q. Where can one find the nation's first Grand Lodge Masonic library?

A. Cedar Rapids.

Q. The State Historical Society of Iowa published what popular journal from 1921 to 1995?

A. The *Palimpsest.*

Q. Early in his career, what author, who refused a Pulitzer Prize for fiction in 1926, was briefly a reporter for the *Waterloo Courier*?

A. Sinclair Lewis.

Q. What youth organization's handbook was extensively revised in 1990 by Bob Birkby, a Fremont County native?

A. The Boy Scouts of America.

Q. A fourth-generation journalist, what Greenfield native joined the staff of *Life* in 1955, then switched to *Time* in 1957?

A. Hugh Sidey.

Q. What is the name of Claes Oldenberg's sculpture in Des Moines's Nollen Plaza?

A. *The Crusoe Umbrella.*

Q. Mark Twain, a temporary resident, believed the sunsets in what Iowa town were without equal?

A. Muscatine.

Q. What percentage of Iowans can read and write?

A. 99 percent (highest in the United States).

Q. Beginning in 1928, what newspaper was among the first in the nation to use airplanes for news gathering?

A. The *Des Moines Register and Tribune.*

Q. What was the profession of the man who gave Grant Wood his start by allowing him to live in his garage in Cedar Rapids?

A. Undertaker.

Q. What advice columnists are twin sisters born in Sioux City on the Fourth of July in 1918?

A. Ann Landers and Abigail Van Buren.

Q. What senior pastor at the Crystal Cathedral in Golden Grove, California, and host of television's *Hour of Power,* was born in Alton in 1926?

A. Robert Schuller.

Q. What Osage author won the 1922 Pulitzer Prize for *A Daughter of the Middle Border* in his autobiographical series?

A. Hamlin Garland.

Q. In 1990 what percentage of the student body at Grinnell College studied Russian?

A. 10 percent.

Q. How much did the Art Institute of Chicago pay for Grant Wood's painting *American Gothic*?

A. Three hundred dollars.

Q. Fort Dodge native Thomas Heggen wrote what novel that became a play and a film starring Henry Fonda?

A. *Mister Roberts.*

Q. What Newton author, an advocate of conservation, was largely responsible for the passage of a congressional act to save the buffalo in Yellowstone National Park?

A. Emerson Hough.

Q. What novel describing the horrors of a Confederate prison camp won Webster City native MacKinlay Kantor a 1955 Pulitzer Prize?

A. *Andersonville.*

Q. How many arts fairs and festivals are held annually in the state?

A. More than 160.

Q. Where was the site of the first small-town independent Chautauqua in Iowa?

A. Allerton.

Q. In 1920 Cornell became the first academic institution to invite what poet to lecture and read his works?

A. Carl Sandburg.

Q. The Iowa state capitol is an excellent example of what type of architecture?

A. Romanesque.

Q. What Mason City native as editorial cartoonist for the *Denver Post* and the *Los Angeles Times* won three Pulitzer Prizes?

A. Paul Conrad.

Q. Named at birth Roy Frowick, what New York fashion designer was born in Des Moines and attended Roosevelt High School there?

A. Roy Halston.

Q. What Grammy- and Academy Award-winning jazz musician earned his bachelor of arts degree at Grinnell College?

A. Herbie Hancock.

Q. What prolific author of such books as *Tales of the South Pacific, Centennial,* and *Hawaii* studied at the University of Iowa Writers' Workshop?

A. James A. Michener.

Q. Born in Sibley in 1914, what author wrote the mystery novels *Cooking School Murders, Baked Bean Supper Murders,* and *The Nantucket Diet Murders*?

A. Virginia G. Rich.

Q. The 1972 Pulitzer Prize for fiction was won by what Lake Mills native for *Angle of Repose*?

A. Wallace Stegner.

Q. What Woodbury County native is the official portrait artist for Jimmy Carter and has drawn covers for *Time* magazine?

A. Robert Templeton.

Q. What Davenport native wrote the book *Old Ironsides* and was editor of the *World Almanac* from 1948 to 1965?

A. Harry Hansen.

Q. Who designed Cedar Rock, a home of Usonian architecture, in Quasqueton?

A. Frank Lloyd Wright.

Q. The Iowa State campus includes several sculptures by what artist-in-residence from 1937 to 1955?

A. Christian Petersen.

Q. What former Sheldon resident wrote the books *A Literary History of Iowa, Growing Up in Iowa,* and *Christmas in Iowa*?

A. Clarence Andrews.

Q. What Wiota farmer became one of the most popular writers of dime novels in the late 1880s with such titles as *Hawkeye Harry* and *Tiger Tom, the Texas Terror*?

A. Oll Coomes.

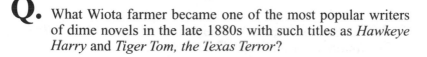

Q. What Emmetsburg native was a managing editor of both the *New York Globe* and the *New Republic*?

A. Bruce Bliven.

Q. Who wrote *One Foot in Heaven,* a bestseller about a minister's life in fictionized Riverton (modeled after Burlington)?

A. Hartzell Spence.

Q. Spending the summer of 1893 in Spillville, what composer made final revisions of his *New World Symphony*?

A. Anton Dvořák.

Q. Grant Wood established what artists' colony in 1932?

A. Stone City.

Q. At the height of his career, what *Des Moines Register* editorial cartoonist, syndicated through the *New York Tribune,* was enjoyed daily by millions of Americans?

A. Jay N. "Ding" Darling.

Q. The annual Rosemaling Exhibition is held in conjunction with what other festival?

A. Nordic Fest.

Q. Where was Honore Willsie Morrow, author of *With Malice Toward None* and *Mary Todd Lincoln,* born in 1880?

A. Ottumwa.

Q. What Montour native wrote biographies of Harry S. Truman, Lyndon Johnson, and Dwight D. Eisenhower?

A. Merle Miller.

Q. What Winterset native founded *Redbook* magazine?

A. Turnbull White.

Q. Who composed "The Missouri Waltz"?

A. Frederick Knight Logan, an Iowa native.

Q. Besides being authors, what do Flannery O'Connor and John Irving have in common?

A. Both studied at the University of Iowa Writers' Workshop.

Q. In what city in 1995 was the North American Bible Quiz Tournament held?

A. Des Moines.

Q. What is the state's oldest continuing newspaper?

A. The *Hawk Eye.*

Q. W. P. Kinsella wrote the novel *Shoeless Joe,* which served as the basis for what movie?

A. *Field of Dreams.*

Q. What Cedar Rapids resident was instrumental in ushering in the golden era of the circuit Chautauqua (a literary/musical forum) in 1904?

A. Keith Vawter.

Q. What Burnside native authored *Ballad to an Iowa Farmer and Other Reflections* and won a Pulitzer Prize for his national reporting on Jimmy Hoffa in 1958?

A. Clark Raymond Mollenhoff.

Q. Who wrote "The Song of Iowa"?
A. Maj. S. H. M. Byers.

Q. What was the first permanent art facility built in Iowa?
A. Blanden Memorial Art Museum in Fort Dodge.

Q. In what town is the house that served as the backdrop in Grant Wood's painting *American Gothic*?

A. Eldon.

Q. Where is Iowa's oldest continually running theater?
A. Story City.

Q. What Adams County native founded and edited *Midland: A Magazine of the Middle West* from 1915 to 1933, and conducted the CBS radio program *Of Books and Men* in the 1930s and 1940s?

A. John T. Frederick.

Q. Although Harriet Ketcham of Mount Pleasant designed the Iowa Soldiers and Sailors Monument on the state capitol grounds, what sculptor completed the work?

A. Carl Rohl-Smith, after Ketcham's death.

Q. What prolific author, the uncle of tycoon Howard Hughes, spent his boyhood in Keokuk?

A. Rupert Hughes.

Q. At the turn of the century, what Estherville man patented a process for painting theatrical scenery by using dye?

A. Jesse Cox.

Q. How many daily newspapers did Iowa have as of 1995?

A. Forty-one.

Q. By 1905, with only 184 towns with a population of more than one thousand, Iowa had how many opera houses?

A. 122.

Q. What was the most unusual attraction at Ottumwa's Coal Palace in 1890 and 1891?

A. A miniature mine.

Q. What Iowa cartoonist was appointed head of the U.S. Biological Service by Franklin D. Roosevelt?

A. J. N. "Ding" Darling.

Q. In what year did Iowa-based *Look* magazine cease publication?

A. 1971.

Q. The 1992 Pulitzer Prize for fiction went to what University of Iowa alumnus for *A Thousand Acres*?

A. Jane Smiley.

Q. What long-time *Chicago Daily News* drama critic was born in West Burlington and during the 1880s was famous as opera singer Lillie West?

A. Amy Leslie.

Q. What 1980 Pulitzer Prize-winning poet earned his doctorate at the University of Iowa in 1954?

A. Donald Justice.

Q. What county's courthouse is modeled after the Château Azay-le-Rideaux in the Loire Valley of France?

A. Dallas.

Q. Students and staff from Stephens College of Columbia, Missouri, put on professional plays each year at what theater?

A. Okoboji Summer Theatre.

Q. What architect designed a house for Dr. George C. Stockman in Mason City in 1908?

A. Frank Lloyd Wright.

Q. What well-known Iowan wrote such books as *Principles of Mining, American Individualism,* and *American Epic*?

A. Herbert Hoover.

Q. What Shenandoah native, a writer at the *Des Moines Register* since 1972, is known as "the Iowa Boy"?

A. Chuck Offenburger.

Q. Where is the world's largest collection of Grant Wood artwork?

A. Cedar Rapids Museum of Art.

Q. After it moved from Fort Madison in 1839, where is the *Hawk Eye* published today?

A. Burlington.

Q. What artist and illustrator, whose clients include *The New Yorker, Rolling Stone,* and *Cosmopolitan,* has his studio on Main Street in Cedar Falls?

A. Gary Kelley.

Q. What was historian Benjamin Shambaugh's nickname during his time in Iowa City?

A. Mr. History of Iowa.

Q. What former director of the Iowa Historical Department, Museum and Archives Division, with his wife wrote *Waterfowl of Iowa,* which was illustrated by Maynard Reece?

A. Jack Musgrove.

Q. In a public expression of thanks for a bountiful harvest, what edifice was built in Sioux City in 1887?

A. A corn palace.

———◆———

Q. What was the relationship between Grant Wood and the man who served as the model in *American Gothic*?

A. He was Wood's dentist.

———◆———

Q. What 1935 novel by MacKinlay Kantor is the tale of a fox hunter's hound?

A. *The Voice of Bugle Ann.*

———◆———

Q. Lois Lenski wrote what 1954 children's book about an eleven-year-old boy living on an Iowa farm?

A. *Corn-Farm Boy.*

Q. What Cascade-born Baseball Hall of Famer was the last Chicago White Sox pitcher to win twenty-five games in a season?

A. Red Faber.

Q. What All-Star catcher who played most of his major-league career with the Texas Rangers is a University of Iowa graduate?

A. Jim Sundberg.

Q. Davenport Central High School's Roger Craig was a star running back for what NFL team most of his career?

A. The San Francisco 49ers.

Q. What town is host to the annual Tri-State Rodeo?

A. Fort Madison.

Q. Nicknamed "the Roland Rocket," who was the first two-sport All-American at Iowa State?

A. Gary Thompson (basketball and baseball).

Q. Iowa State All-American Matt Blair was drafted by what NFL team?

A. Minnesota Vikings.

Q. In 1896 the first five-player basketball game west of the Mississippi was held at what school?

A. University of Iowa.

Q. Prof. Frank D. Paine chose the name *VEISHEA* in 1922 for the Iowa State University celebration by using the first letters of what five divisions of the college?

A. Veterinary, Engineering, Industrial Science, Home Economics, and Agriculture.

Q. Who are the only two football players to have had their numbers retired by the University of Iowa?

A. Nile Kinnick (24) and Cal Jones (62).

Q. What museum near Okoboji features restored boats?

A. Iowa Great Lakes Maritime Museum.

Q. A pro football player for both the New York Jets and the Kansas City Chiefs, Searsboro's Jeff Criswell is a 1986 graduate of what college?

A. Graceland.

Q. What Scranton native and former Northern Iowa player was named the NFL's 1995 defensive player of the year as a linebacker for the Buffalo Bills?

A. Bryce Paup.

Q. Where is the Iowa Championship Rodeo held?

A. Sidney.

Q. What college won the Women's Softball College World Series in 1977?

A. University of Northern Iowa.

SCIENCE & NATURE

C H A P T E R   S I X

Q. What town is famous for its cereal mills?

A. Cedar Rapids.

Q. In what year was the first railroad bridge built across the Mississippi River?

A. 1856.

Q. What type of trees were planted on the grounds of the U.S. Capitol on June 12, 1952, in memory of the five Sullivan brothers who died in 1942 during an attack on the USS *Juneau* in the Solomon Islands?

A. Crab apple.

Q. What percentage of Iowa's commodities are transported via motor freight carriers?

A. 75 percent.

Q. What Spencer woman is credited with creating the word *blizzard* in 1868 after reading a story about a man named Mr. Blizzard who had a raging temper?

A. Lephe Wells Coates.

Q. At what school did George Washington Carver receive a bachelor's degree in science?

A. Iowa State Agricultural College and Model Farm (now Iowa State University of Science and Technology).

Q. Iowa ranked first nationally in the production of what two crops in 1900?

A. Corn and oats.

Q. What city at one time had seven plants for manufacturing clayware and thus was considered the brick and tile capital of the world?

A. Mason City.

Q. What is the Iowa record amount of snowfall for one day?

A. Twenty-four inches, April 20, 1918, in Lenox.

Q. What term was used to describe the resistance of farmers to the testing of dairy cattle by state veterinarians in 1931?

A. Cow War.

Q. How many different types of fish are found in Iowa?

A. 149.

Q. Early settlers discovered what type of animal bones in a narrow ravine called Boneyard Hollow, now part of Dolliver State Park?

A. Buffalo.

Q. What underground river cavern is near McGregor?

A. Spook Cave.

Q. How many tornadoes does Iowa average a year?

A. Thirty-four.

Q. In 1895 what health-care therapy originated in Davenport?

A. Chiropractic.

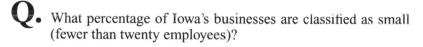

Q. What percentage of Iowa's businesses are classified as small (fewer than twenty employees)?

A. 90 percent.

Q. Situated in Dubuque, what is the world's steepest and shortest railway?

A. Fenelon Place Elevator.

Q. What was the first car to have four-wheel hydraulic brakes?

A. Duesenberg Model A.

Q. Graduating seniors and faculty members of Wartburg College plant what flowers on campus after each spring's baccalaureate service?

A. Marigolds.

Q. Where is the oldest water tower still in service in Iowa?

A. Scranton.

Q. Where was the first light bulb in the state, purchased for a mine in Cleveland, Iowa, actually turned on?

A. Lucas.

Q. Astronauts David C. Hilmers, George "Pinky" Nelson, and Dale Garner were all residents of what county?

A. Clinton.

Q. In 1993 what was the value of the average farm acre?

A. $1,275.

Q. As a division of Winnebago Industries, what company is the largest television network in the nation, sending TV commercials from advertising agencies to TV stations via satellite?

A. Cycle Sat.

Q. Mineral water from what town was sent in barrels to the White House by order of President Grover Cleveland's physician?

A. Colfax.

Q. What Iowa State University professor is considered the father of the electronic digital computer?

A. John Vincent Atanasoff.

Q. In 1938 the Adams Ranch in Sac County was the largest single block of farmland in the state with how many acres?

A. More than seven thousand.

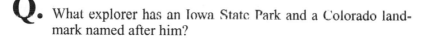

Q. Who invented a flying machine similar to a helicopter in Imogene in 1886?

A. August Werner.

Q. What explorer has an Iowa State Park and a Colorado landmark named after him?

A. Zebulon Pike.

Q. Motor Mill, southeast of Elkader and the tallest mill in the Midwest, is constructed of what material?

A. Native limestone.

Q. How many stories tall is the Principal Financial Group Building in Des Moines?

A. Forty-four.

Q. A children's hospital was added to the University of Iowa Hospitals in what year?

A. 1919.

Q. What type of road was built between Mount Pleasant and Burlington in the mid-1800s?

A. Plank.

Q. Muscatine Island is most noted for what fruit?

A. Watermelon.

Q. What did Iowan Charles Osborne do every 1.5 seconds from 1922 until February 1990?

A. Hiccup.

Q. How much revenue do Iowa's four thousand manufacturing firms gross annually?

A. More than $10.5 billion.

Q. What Iowa lake is one of the three "blue lakes" in the world?

A. West Okoboji.

Q. What fuels the majority of steam generators in Iowa's eighty-one power plants?

A. Coal.

Q. What wildlife refuge contains nearly eight thousand acres of the Missouri River floodplain between Iowa and Nebraska?

A. DeSoto National Wildlife Refuge.

Q. What is the average temperature in August, Iowa's warmest month?

A. 72.1 degrees Fahrenheit.

Q. Who made the first recorded airplane flight in Iowa on May 10, 1910?

A. Arthur J. Hartman.

Q. In 1993 what was the average size of an Iowa farm?

A. 333 acres.

Q. What percentage of Iowa is forest?

A. 4 percent.

Q. The master clock that controls other clocks in the state capitol must be wound once a week and is operated by what power?

A. Air.

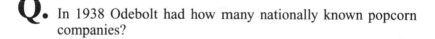

Q. In 1938 Odebolt had how many nationally known popcorn companies?

A. Three (J. L. Bruce Popcorn Company, Albert Dickinson Popcorn Company, and Cracker Jack Popcorn Company).

Q. Iowa is number one in the nation in raising what farm animals?

A. Pigs.

Q. In what type of aircraft did Nickolas Piantanida set a world record for highest altitude, at 123,800 feet?

A. Helium balloon.

Q. Fort Dodge is one of the world's leading makers of products made from what mineral?

A. Gypsum.

Q. During the Civil War, Keokuk's Annie Wittenmyer was instrumental in establishing what facilities in army hospitals?

A. Diet kitchens.

Q. In what year did the Quaker Oats Company begin making Life cereal?

A. 1958.

Q. In 1879 Kalona had a shorthorn breeding service that earned what nickname for the town?

A. Bulltown.

Q. What Iowa county has the highest percentage of grade-A topsoil in the nation?

A. Wright.

Q. Iowa has how many state forests?

A. Nine.

Q. What 1935 Iowa State alumnus developed the first single-cross hybrid corn for volume production?

A. Raymond Baker.

Q. In 1891 a large glacial boulder found in Black Hawk County was used to construct what building in Waterloo?

A. Boulder Church.

Q. What state park contains thirteen limestone caves and a natural bridge?

A. Maquoketa.

Q. Who designed the first flexible door hanger and monorail conveyor system in 1919 in Fairfield?

A. William Louden.

Q. Where is the production center of Hy-Line International, the world's largest producer of breeding stock for egg-laying chickens?

A. Dallas Center.

Q. What was the first man-made lake in Iowa?

A. Pine Lake.

Q. How much of Iowa's land was given to railroad companies?

A. About 10 percent.

Q. Born in Des Moines in 1877, who invented the electric razor?

A. Jacob Schick.

Q. What is considered the greatest natural disaster in Iowa's history?

A. The flood of 1993.

Q. What is the average annual rainfall in Iowa?

A. Thirty-two inches.

Q. What percentage of the nation's corn is grown in Iowa?

A. 20 percent.

Q. Where is the Exploratorium of Iowa located?

A. Ottumwa.

Q. Who invented an "electricity machine" in Perry but died before he could display how it worked?

A. Henry Nelson.

Q. Between what two cities did the first railroad begin operating?

A. Davenport and Muscatine.

Q. During the summer of 1936, Allamakee County offered a bounty of fifty cents for three inches of tail from what creatures?

A. Rattlesnakes.

Q. In what year was the Iowa Board of Veterinary Medicine created?

A. 1900.

Q. How much do the sheets of twenty-three-carat gold on the dome of the Iowa capitol weigh?

A. One hundred ounces each.

Q. George Gallup, the statistician who established opinion-poll-sampling techniques, was born in 1901 in what town?

A. Jefferson.

Q. Where was the world's first academic program linking veterinary medicine and electrical engineering (called biomedical engineering) established?

A. Iowa State University.

Q. Where is the world's largest roller dam located?

A. Davenport.

Q. Clam shells found at the bend of a river near Muscatine led to what industry?

A. Pearl button making.

Q. Loras College has the world's largest live collection of what algae?

A. Diatoms.

Q. In 1880 what Waterloo resident became the first president of AT&T?

A. Theodore Vail.

Q. Using the fruits, vegetables, and blossoms of rhubarb, dandelion, red clover, and cherry, what is produced in Amana?

A. Wine.

Q. A telephone museum can be found in what Iowa town?

A. Jefferson.

Q. The wreck of what 1864 steamboat can be seen at the DeSoto National Wildlife Refuge?

A. The *Bertrand*.

Q. A large bird's nest in a grove of oak trees above the Boone River gave what town its name?

A. Eagle Grove.

Q. Where does Iowa rank nationally in livestock and livestock products?

A. Second (behind only Texas).

Q. Where was the first rotary pump built?

A. Cedar Falls.

Q. In 1920 what company was established when Henry A. Wallace and his partner Jay J. Newlin began to raise hybridized seed corn to sell near Johnston?

A. Pioneer Hi-bred International, Inc.

Q. In 1938 farmers from what county were the first to produce electricity on farmer-owned lines?

A. Franklin.

Q. What is Iowa's average annual snowfall?

A. Thirty-two inches.

Q. How tall was the world's tallest corn stalk, grown by Don Radda of Washington in 1946?

A. Thirty-one feet, three inches.

Q. What is the state's record high temperature?

A. 118 degrees Fahrenheit, in Keokuk on July 20, 1934.

Q. Born on a farm near Provitin, who was the only agriculturalist to win a Nobel Peace Prize?

A. Dr. Norman Borlaug.

Q. On the bluffs of what river is one of only three locations in the world where cliff-dwelling pigeons can be found?

A. Iowa River.

Q. The panic of 1873, coupled with a plague of what insect, led to the closing of the mills in Milford?

A. Grasshoppers.

Q. How many acres of Iowa are farmland?

A. 33.5 million.

Q. When a dike broke after torrential rains in 1986, Crystal Lake, a thirty-five-acre lake near DeWitt, drained in how many minutes?

A. Fifteen.

Q. What county had the first tax-supported hospital in the nation?

A. Washington.

Q. What is the last name of the father and son who invented and developed chiropractic?

A. Palmer.

Q. For what invention did Dubuque's John L. Harvey receive a patent in 1856?

A. Paper clip.

Q. What percentage of Iowa land is arable?

A. 94 percent.

Q. What type of tree near Perry, rated the finest of its species by the Iowa Federated Garden Clubs in 1936, started as a fishing pole stuck in the ground?

A. Cottonwood.

Q. What is the largest cereal factory in the world?

A. Quaker Oats.

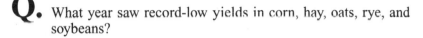

Q. What year saw record-low yields in corn, hay, oats, rye, and soybeans?

A. 1934.

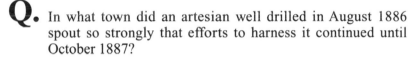

Q. In what town did an artesian well drilled in August 1886 spout so strongly that efforts to harness it continued until October 1887?

A. Belle Plaine.

Q. How many different varieties of ferns have been found in Wildcat Den State Park near Muscatine?

A. Twenty-five.

Q. In 1973 East Lake Park in Osceola was deeded to Clarke County for how much money?

A. One dollar.

Q. When was the first recorded earthquake in Iowa?

A. January 4, 1843.

Q. What national figure planted a tree in the park in Keokuk in 1903?

A. President Theodore Roosevelt.

Q. What is the state rock?

A. Geode.

Q. Developed at the University of Iowa, the nationally administered Iowa Test of Basic Skills was first given Iowa school children in what year?

A. 1935.

Q. In 1910 what Iowan became the first person to make a ship-to-shore flight in an airplane?

A. Eugene B. Ely.

Q. What Cedar Rapids physician developed x-ray treatment for cancer?

A. Arthur Erskine.

Q. In 1835 who described tall prairie grass in central Iowa as so high that it "could be tied in knots over the horses' backs"?

A. Lt. Col. Stephen Kearney.

Q. A fossil park in the open pits of a former brick and tile plant is near what town?

A. Rockford.

Q. Where is Iowa's only fire tower situated?

A. Yellow River State Forest.

◆

Q. Founded in 1954, Ida Grove's Midwest Industries, Inc., developed what type of equipment used in one form on farms and in another form on waterfronts?

A. Hoist.

◆

Q. In 1989 Iowa ranked first nationally in the production of hogs, corn, and what other grain crop?

A. Oats.

◆

Q. In what year did Maytag produce its last wringer washing machines?

A. 1983.

◆

Q. In what Amana village is Amana Refrigeration, Inc., headquartered?

A. Middle Amana.

◆

Q. Robert N. Noyce, who invented the microchip and received the National Medal of Science, was a graduate of what college?

A. Grinnell.

◆

Q. What was the second town west of the Mississippi to have electric lighting and was the first to have a public power system?

A. Fairfield.

Q. What is Iowa's chief fruit crop?

A. Apples.

Q. Spirit Lake is especially noted for what type of fish?

A. Pike.

Q. George Washington Carver taught what subject for two years at Iowa State?

A. Botany.

Q. What is the average annual temperature in Iowa?

A. Forty-eight degrees Fahrenheit.

Q. What is the state bird?

A. Eastern goldfinch.

Q. What Des Moines man built the first successful electric car in the United States and demonstrated it in 1888?

A. William Morrison.

Q. With eight women in its class, the University of Iowa's medical department became the first coeducational medical school in what year?

A. 1870.

Q. The purchase of what 240-acre state preserve by the Iowa Conservation Commission in 1945 was the beginning of the state's prairie protection efforts?

A. Hayden Prairie.

Q. What physicist—born, educated, and employed in Iowa in 1958 discovered the radiation belts that circle the earth, which were named for him?

A. James A. Van Allen (Van Allen radiation belts).

Q. The University of Iowa Hospitals at Iowa City was established in what year?

A. 1898.

Q. Aside from the fur trade, what was the state's first business enterprise?

A. Lead mining.

Q. About how many bushels of corn are grown annually in Iowa?

A. 1.25 billion.

Q. What is normally the rainiest month?

A. June.

Q. What national wildlife refuge is the watershed for both the Blue Earth and Des Moines Rivers and therefore has water that runs both north and south?

A. Union Slough in Kossuth County.

Q. Near what town is the Kate Shelley High Bridge, one of the world's highest double-track railroad bridges?

A. Boone.

Q. For what cheese is the Maytag Dairy Farm especially noted?

A. Maytag Blue Cheese.

Q. What company in Cedar Rapids utilizes a large share of Iowa's oat crop?

A. Quaker Oats.

Q. What Latimer dentist invented the plastic eye?

A. Dr. Milton Wirtz.

Q. The Pleasant Creek Recreation Area has the most northerly stand of what kind of tree in the Western Hemisphere?

A. Pecan.

Q. Where was the first statistical laboratory in the nation?

A. Iowa State University.

Q. What pioneer aviator from Denison broke the long-distance record set by Lindbergh and also flew the first transatlantic mail flight in 1927?

A. Clarence D. Chamberlin.

Q. What Council Bluffs-born inventor patented the vacuum tube, basic to the development of long-distance radio and television communication?

A. Dr. Lee De Forest.

Q. Who gave Pella's Formal Tulip Gardens its first twenty-five thousand bulbs?

A. The Holland Flower Bulb Growers Association.

Q. What is the state flower?
A. Wild rose.

Q. A rare earthquake tremor measuring between four and five on the Richter scale shook parts of eastern Iowa in what year?

A. 1972.

Q. What corporation is the world's second-largest window and door manufacturer?

A. Pella Corporation.

Q. In what town is the Bily Clock Museum located?
A. Spillville.

Q. Where does Iowa rank nationally in farm income?
A. Third (behind No. 1 California and No. 2 Texas).

Q. How many apples did the Delicious apple tree bear during its first year of production?

A. One.

Q. Iowa has had more recorded tornadoes than any other state except which one?

A. Kansas.

Q. The meat-packing industry in Sioux City started by accident after a boat containing what product sank in the Missouri River?

A. Wheat.

Q. What material comprised the tables used in Iowa's first glass schoolhouse?

A. Chemically treated hard rubber.

Q. What was the record rainfall for one day, which occurred in Larrabee in Cherokee County on June 24, 1891?

A. 12.99 inches.

Q. Dr. Robert Millikan, born in Maquoketa in 1868, was the first American to win the Nobel Prize in what field?

A. Physics.

Q. Where is the state's only long-range radar station located?

A. Arlington.

Q. Situated in Davenport, what was the first hospital built in Iowa?

A. Mercy Hospital.

◆

Q. Besides gravel and gypsum, what is the other nonfuel substance produced in Iowa?

A. Portland cement.

◆

Q. What is the principal poultry raised in Iowa?

A. Turkey.

◆

Q. In what year did Quaker Oats begin producing Cap'n Crunch cereal?

A. 1963.

◆

Q. What Iowa town bills itself as the home of the world's largest horse sale?

A. Waverly.

◆

Q. Rainwater falling on the east side of what county courthouse eventually flows into the Mississippi River, while that falling on the west side flows into the Missouri River?

A. Lucas County Courthouse in Chariton.

◆

Q. What cave near Dubuque contains formations known as anthodites or cave flowers?

A. Crystal Lake Cave.

Q. What Iowa farmer, one of the world's largest producers of hybrid seed corn, shared his knowledge of good farming methods with Russia in the midst of the Cold War?

A. Roswell Garst.

◆

Q. Iowa is one of how many states with two world-class research universities?

A. Four.

◆

Q. Expected to be completed around 2004, what is the name of the network of highways crossing Iowa that will connect Saint Louis and Saint Paul?

A. Avenue of the Saints.

◆

Q. Dr. Lucy Hobbs, who lived in McGregor from 1862 to 1865, was the first woman to receive what degree?

A. Doctor of Dental Surgery.

◆

Q. Estherville is the site of one of the largest meteorites on record which crashed two miles north of the city on May 10 of what year?

A. 1879.

◆

Q. Christian K. Nelson invented what ice cream novelty?

A. Eskimo Pies.

◆

Q. Situated two and one-half miles southwest of Strawberry Point, what is Iowa's oldest state park?

A. Backbone.

Q. On May 15 of what year did a tornado hit Charles City, destroying 265 businesses, 1,203 homes, and 1,250 cars, and killing 13 people?

A. 1968.

Q. Fort Dodge, known as Gypsum City since 1872, has how many modern gypsum plants?

A. Four.

Q. How many species of birds are found in Iowa?

A. 227.

Q. In what year did the U.S. Weather Bureau begin keeping statistical records in Iowa?

A. 1873.

Q. In what year did Thomas Macbride form the Iowa Park and Forestry Association?

A. 1901.

Q. In 1903 what town became home to the largest railroad shop west of the Mississippi River?

A. Bettendorf.

Q. What is Iowa's most valuable crop export?

A. Soybeans.

Q. What is the state's record low temperature?

A. Minus forty-seven degrees Fahrenheit, in Washta on January 12, 1912.

Q. Who was appointed the first national director of boys' and girls' club work (later called 4-H) in the U.S. Department of Agriculture?

A. O. H. Benson.

Q. What is the largest pork-producing county in the world?

A. Delaware.

Q. What company in Cresco is the nation's leading builder of aluminum livestock, horse, and utility trailers?

A. Feather-Lite Trailers.

Q. How many pounds of fish are commercially caught in Iowa each year?

A. Three million.

Q. What is the number-one game bird in the state?

A. Pheasant.

Q. The disciplines of educational testing and speech pathology began at what institution?

A. University of Iowa.

Q. Situated in Muscatine, what is the largest canning plant between the Mississippi River and the Rocky Mountains?

A. H. J. Heinz Company.

Q. Where are the home offices for the world's largest popcorn producer (American Popcorn) and the nation's largest honey co-op (Sue Bee Honey)?

A. Sioux City.

Q. In what year did a tornado kill fifteen people south of DeWitt, continuing on its path of destruction and death to Camanche?

A. 1860.

Q. What is the largest coal-producing county in the state?

A. Marion.

Q. How many state parks are in Iowa?

A. Eighty-three.

Q. Large artesian wells beneath the town gave Goldfield what nickname?

A. Fountain City.

Q. During the flood of 1993, for how many days was the entire city of Des Moines without drinking water?

A. Twenty.

Q. What is the state tree?

A. Oak.

Q. Iowa contains what percentage of all the first-class farmland in the United States?

A. 25 percent.

Q. Situated at Fort Madison, what is the name of the largest double-deck, swing-span bridge in the world?

A. Santa Fe Bridge.

Q. What two crops make up more than 94 percent of the total value of production in the state?

A. Corn and soybeans.

Q. What laboratory was established by Thomas H. Macbride for "the study of nature in nature"?

A. Iowa Lakeside Laboratory.

Q. What county has the most acreage of apple orchards?

A. Harrison.

Q. Where is the home of Wells' Dairy, best known for Blue Bunny products?

A. Le Mars.

Q. What is the only natural substance that can be restored to its original rocklike state by adding water?

A. Gypsum.

Q. January, the coldest month, averages what temperature?

A. 17.3 degrees Fahrenheit.

Q. What Iowa State scientist and his associates developed an economical method of extracting uranium from uranium fluoride?

A. Dr. Frank Spedding.

Q. What percentage of Iowa's food production is sold to foreign buyers?

A. About 25 percent.

Q. What ten-foot-high clock is in Spillville?

A. The American Pioneer History Clock.

Q. What county has a state hatchery that raises quail and pheasants?

A. Boone.

Q. What is Iowa's gross annual farm income?

A. $11 billion.

Q. In 1994 what Maharishi University of Management professor returned more than $600,000 in federal grant money on the ethical grounds his DNA research might lead to dangerous applications?

A. Dr. John Fagan.

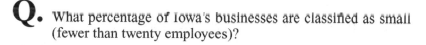

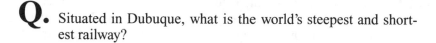

